Deborah Gol

olivemount™
press
Carlsbad, CA 92009

I can I will I believe

1st edition
1 December 2003
First Printing

ISBN 097156384-5

9 780971 563841

Printed in the U.S.A.

Providence Systems, Inc.®
ClubNet®
I can, I will, I believe™
Mastermind Summit™
Oh, by the way...™
Peak Performers™
Turning Point Retreats™
are registered trademarks of Providence Systems, Inc., Carlsbad, CA 92009

Dedication

To Brian and the A-Team
Anthony, Anna, Alex, Adam, Amy, and Alysha
and to my Father and Mother
James and Julia Robinson

You are the reason for this book.

Its purpose is personal...to let each of you know that realizing your dreams is only a mindset away. My own life convinces me that every one of us is given the opportunity to make our dreams and goals come true.

I believe, and you should believe, your significance in the grand design of life. In sharing with you my experiences and beliefs, I hope to help you realize your own abilities and importance...encourage you in your journey toward a better, fuller life...and urge you on in your efforts to become the best that you can be. By relating my own motivation and methodology, I seek to offer assistance in overcoming obstacles, meeting challenges, achieving goals and attaining personal success.

That is my goal and my message. If you gain inspiration from these pages, it will be fulfilling, but will have come from a greater source than me.

I welcome you into my life, my thoughts, and the encouragement you may draw from my words.

CHAPTER 1

You can, and I can help you.

"You can do it."

Every parent in the world has encouraged a child with these words. Every coach has said it to every player. Every friend has said these words to a friend who has in turn said them to another friend. These words are shouted when we are striving for success or competing for a triumphant win, and they are muttered while we overcome adversity. Sometimes accompanied by tears, it's what we whisper to ourselves while we watch rescuers save someone from a life-or-death situation or when we root for anyone who is in peril.

You can do it applies to all human endeavor, from a toddler's first steps on the living room floor to Neil Armstrong's "giant leap for mankind" on the moon.

What child has not felt uplifted and supported by hearing it? What friend or athlete or person in peril has not welcomed these words? They are the spoken essence of the human spirit, words of encouragement and faith. They inspire us to accomplish, and they require belief...in ourselves, in others, and in a Greater Power than ourselves. The phrase also presents us at our best...believing in, caring for, and wishing success for another. In a sense, it is a fulfillment of the Golden Rule, which directs us to do unto others as we would have others do unto us.

Because the words are so inspiring and meaningful to us in our earliest strivings and so reinforcing and encouraging throughout our lives, they make up a powerful motivating message for all of us personally. Along with *I love you*, the phrase *You can do it* is as positive and motivating as anything another person can say to you.

You can do it is at the root of my own philosophy for personal accomplishment. Since I believe in the power of positive self-talk...and in God-inspired factors other than pure self-reliance...I have expanded the concept and the words into *I can, I will, I believe*. These declarations bring the necessary faith in God and self into the equation and strengthen an individual's commitment and purpose. They also turn the encouragement from objective, coming from someone else, to subjective, growing from within yourself as self-encouragement and dedication to accomplishment.

This is my idea: to make *You can do it* work for yourself with the help of God and without the need for it to be said to you by another person. It is extremely important to me that the strength to accomplish come from within oneself.

I've heard *You can do it* stated many ways in my life. The precise wording is not a critical issue; the concepts are supremely important. My father is an excellent example of this. He had a slightly different approach and a slightly different way of declaring his own positive commitment, belief in self, and dedication to accomplishment. But it boiled down to the same thing. His way was learned from his father who would ask him when my father faced a difficult task, "Can you do it?" My dad's answer would be, "Yes, I can." And his father would say, "Okay then…" This exchange took place over and over again as my dad grew up.

Because it was ingrained in him, my father often used this same exchange with us. One of my earliest memories of its effectiveness was when I was about seven years old and eager to swim in the deep end of the pool. I was clinging to the side of the pool with my feet dangling in the deeper, bluer water near the diving board. Dad looked me in the eyes and said, "Can you do it?" I responded with the magically empowering answer, "Yes, I can," and he said, "Okay then..." So I pushed off and went down deep. I stayed down, trying to figure out how to get back up to the surface. Later, my dad told me he was getting very nervous because I was down for so long. As he was about to dive in and pull me out, I popped up with a huge smile on my face...and with an immense sense of accomplishment. And from that moment, he never had to come with me again when I went to the deep end of the pool.

I remember that fondly as a great step in building my own self-confidence, and I love my father for his gentle, positive way of bringing me to do it myself. I often recall it as I encourage my own children to overcome their self-doubts and believe in themselves and their abilities. I think how fortunate I was to have a father who knew the way to give me that self-confidence. And I realize I have a responsibility to pass this legacy on to my own children.

It's all about people, and it's about them getting the best out of themselves. Each of us has been blessed with our own individualized natural gifts and abilities. Every one of us has a distinctive gem within us, a jewel that is peculiarly our own, ready to shine forth. It is simply a matter of knowing how to let these gifts shine.

My life has brought me to a place where I am in a unique position to help people and, more specifically, to help them use their God-given abilities to get the best out of themselves. My mission is to show them how, based on the experiences and beliefs that have formed my own faith-driven philosophy. My passion is for individual excellence; it's about being your best so you can give your best...to yourself, your family, and everyone you know and meet...in any situation where you can contribute meaningfully and make a difference for the better.

My approach is best summed up in a saying I once heard: *In order to get the best out of others, you must go to their best.* And I often reflect on a quote from Charles Dickens, the ennobling writer who gave us *A Christmas Carol* and *A Tale of Two Cities*: *"All of us have wonders hidden in our breasts, only needing circumstances to evoke them."* I embrace this thinking because it glows with strength and hope.

Because of my own experience in international competition, I am cautious wherever there is a tendency to confuse the pursuit of excellence with perfectionism. We all need to know the difference and the boundaries to our striving. Sometimes we have to cross the line and overdo to learn the difference, and sometimes it is a hard lesson learned.

I greatly respect and admire John Wooden, the peerless teacher and basketball coach at UCLA, for his wisdom regarding the proper approach to sports and life.

He dispelled any misconception about perfectionism and made it clear when he told his players: "Perfection is what you're striving for, but perfection is an impossibility. However, striving for perfection is not an impossibility. Do the best you can under the conditions that exist.

This is what counts." Mr. Wooden's teaching was directed toward building champions. It is exceptional instruction with a powerful mindset, with grace and strength.

If you reread and analyze his words, you will see that they're about the pursuit of perfection and the realistic realization that perfection is unattainable. I would like to add the observation that, when you fall short of perfection in your endeavors, you're still winning if you've given it your all-out best.

Being the best that you can be should always be your desired goal. Most people have a hard time achieving this, and they can benefit greatly from valid assistance. Strange as it seems, many have difficulty understanding this, and they need both a wake-up call and a powerful method of proceeding.

So it's about people and the process of them becoming the best they can be. And what's the best way to accomplish this? How do we go about the mental conditioning necessary to achieve this?

It requires that we habituate the process...intentionally make it a reflexive action or habit in our daily living. That also involves realizing how you invest your time physically and mentally. How you spend your time determines your achievements and accomplishments... and the total outcome of your life.

The process of striving to be your best requires more than thinking only in terms of daily routine; it demands constant automatic concentration throughout each waking day...maintaining during the moment-to-moment mental activity that flows constantly throughout the day.

I believe that we are all naturally prone to self-talk which can be either positive, powerful and reassuring, or negative, critical, punishing and self-sabotaging. Whether the self-talk is positive or negative depends on the individual and that person's perspective. Being your best to give your best is a concept fueled by positive thinking. It is derailed by doubt, disbelief and distrust, and any negative aspects weaken the concept, its effectiveness, and the person.

I can, I will, I believe are positive self-talk tools that can be used in virtually any and every situation to make a significant difference for the good in the outcome. I use these declarations constantly throughout the day...to subdue the enemies of my mind or as energizers to motivate me in the most menial tasks. And I have taught myself to use these affirmations to help me overcome any obstacle, adversity or challenge.

These six words have the capability to reprogram the subconscious mind. Simple, yet so profound are these affirmations that they can transform your life.

CHAPTER 2

I can.

The first of these affirmations sets the process of self-achievement in motion. You see or understand or are confronted by something that you feel you should or must do. It can literally be anything large or small...a relatively insignificant task to a great undertaking; an obstacle to overcome or a problem to be solved; something that will make your life better or will help another or will resolve a conflict. By saying, "*I can*," you identify the thing to be done and you initiate the resolve to do it.

The dictionary defines *CAN* as *to be able mentally or spiritually*. Since I believe that everyone is equipped with natural gifts and abilities and with an inherent good, it holds true that each person has what it takes to achieve the life that is designed for them. To be complete and rewarding, each person's life should incorporate not only their natural abilities and skills, but their dreams and goals, and the possibilities or opportunities to realize them. *I can* tells and assures yourself that you are able and ready to do what you must do.

How did I come to make *I can* the initiating affirmation? What brought me to these subjective words from

"*Can you do it?*" and "*You can do it!*" The answer is not simple; it's been a long journey and a lengthy process of development, built on dramatic successes in competitive athletics and in my personal life and tempered by personal obstacles, setbacks, tragedies, and failures. *I can* and the subsequent affirmations, *I will* and *I believe*, have been formed and refined by all of the experiences of my life. That includes the life-experiences of those near and dear to me. It also includes the experiences of hundreds who have sought help and confided in me through their connection to Providence Systems.

The story of how I came to these affirmations goes all the way back to my very beginnings. One of my favorite childhood stories was *The Little Engine That Could.* This book was read to me over and over. It influenced me greatly, and I believe now in retrospect that I preferred it because it simply and beautifully presented the concept of striving for peak performance. It was done in a way a child could relate to and understand, and the story got the message across to the adult readers as well as to the little listeners. I know that the message of *The Little Engine That Could* stayed in my mind, and I think it helped me long-term. I know it filled my subconscious. It is solid foundational material, important to my development, along with my early Bible lessons and the general wisdom I learned from my parents, teachers and coaches.

It is amazing how such inspirational material from early childhood colors your formative years and shapes your later life. I discovered at an early age while competing on various youth athletic teams that I had some athletic gifts and abilities which held exceptional possibilities for me. Realizing this, I trained hard and competed with great tenacity, the product of my natural determination and persistence.

As I entered high school, it was time to decide what sports I should concentrate on. Naturally, I selected those at which I believed I could excel. Because I was tall and fast, throughout high school I attended summer camps for basketball, track, and volleyball. After one of these camps, a well-known volleyball coach from California praised my performance and abilities and encouraged me to pursue the chance to play volleyball beyond high school.

At the time, I wasn't sure I was college material, and the encouragement from someone knowledgeable in the sport provided exactly the boost I needed.

Back home, while training with a friend in our neighborhood gym, I met another coach whose encouragement set me in motion. He had been observing our practice sessions and happened to be an AAU volleyball coach. He was coincidentally in the gym working out by himself, and he joined us in our workouts. After a few sessions, he told me he saw something very special in my performance and said that I definitely had what it takes to play at the college level. He added that he thought there was a good possibility I could obtain an athletic scholarship.

I walked away from that conversation deep in thought, trying to grasp the full implications of what he'd said. I thought: 'Hey, maybe I can do this!' It started things percolating in my mind, and I began to get excited at the possibilities. Reflecting on my high school accomplishments reinforced my conclusion : *Yes, I can.*

When I thought further about pursuing the dream of obtaining a scholarship, I realized that it required a vulnerability on my part that would be difficult for me. Because I was intensely private, competitive and self-reliant by nature, being vulnerable or transparent has never come easily for me. Now, to gain a scholarship, I would have to intentionally put myself in the position of seeking acceptance based on my performance and prepare for rejection.

The summer after my junior year, I swallowed my vulnerability and anxieties and began writing letters to colleges with established volleyball programs. My parents helped immensely. As a matter of fact, I still have the initial rough draft of the letter that my dad so hopefully helped me write. After all the letters went out to all the colleges, we waited and trusted.

Finally, I received a response from the University of Alabama offering me a full scholarship, and I was delighted. The phrase that resounded in my heart and mind was: "Yes, I CAN do this." That I had achieved such a hoped-for outcome seemed miraculous to me. Yes, it had been fueled by my own dreams, but it had actually come about as the result of encouragement from parents, coaches and friends. Yes, it's courageous to step out into the unknown and risk failure and rejection...but because my goals were clear and my mind was focused, my dreams were coming true. Thank God for the kindness and caring of others and for my own determination.

The need to hold fast to my concept of *I can* didn't stop with going to Alabama and making the team. At spring training during my freshman year, my rookie status was a bit intimidating. Preseason training camps are very testing, designed to weed out those who lack the necessary talent and commitment. The mentality is "How far can we push these aspiring athletes?" I had to say to myself, "I can do this," many times.

I didn't know anyone, and the older team members had their own established friendships and groups. However, I soon became friends with the other rookies and developed a special bond with a girl named Elise Lapeyre, who remains a good friend to this day.

Our schedule was demanding. It required great effort to balance classes and study with volleyball practices. Many times I felt overwhelmed and had to fight off the monster of self-doubt. Many times I felt low or lonely or overlooked. Whenever I assessed my situation and resolved that I can do this, it brightened my outlook. The result was always uplifting, strengthening my persistence and belief in myself. That enabled me to continually press forward.

Particularly in my athletic endeavors, I learned to be patient, that success only comes when and if the *I can* attitude endures over time. Giving up was not an option when things got tough. I had to persist if I wanted to make my hopes and dreams a reality. With that mindset, I could achieve my specific goals.

I can was the cornerstone for success. Constantly reprogramming my thinking with that attitude, I reached and exceeded my expectations. Earning honors and making many friends at the University of Alabama, I went on to become one of the top performers in the state. I made good grades by diligence and independent study. By the end of my sophomore year, I was a far cry from the lonely rookie who had showed up at freshman training camp. I was feeling good about myself, girl...but I was in for some severe tests of my youthful flexibility and faith.

After two years at UA, one day before practice, the coach came in and announced to the team that our program was being disbanded. The room became silent as many of the girls realized the loss.

Our team and personal dreams were being shattered by an administrative decision. The coaches encouraged us to keep our dreams alive and look for other opportunities. Although we all vigorously attempted to get the volleyball program reinstated, it was to no avail. That was my first real encounter with massive disappointment. From it, I learned that administrative economic decisions can be very difficult to deal with at the personal level for those affected.

My reaction was to pursue a continued college career playing volleyball somewhere else. Although I loved Alabama, I was an athlete and a player. There were some exceptional programs in the SEC, namely Kentucky, LSU and Tennessee. In particular, when playing against Tennessee, I had observed that this team reflected some qualities that especially appealed to me. The coaches appeared to be exceptionally professional and seemed to have high expectations for the girls. Everything about the Tennessee team showed discipline and winning attitude; even their athletic gear was always lined up and in order. They played tenaciously and had a winning record.

After a lot of thinking and discussion and much prayer, I contacted the University of Tennessee and inquired about joining their program. Once again I was holding on to the edge of the pool, ready to dive into a strange place. It was scary, and once again there was the possibility of rejection. However, my passion to play volleyball was so strong that it overrode any such worries, and my conviction had been reprogrammed with the powerful thinking of *I can*, overriding any self-doubt or self-sabotaging thoughts. These are the benefits of a mental regimen that builds you up instead of tearing you down.

I was able to go forward from disappointment at Alabama to success at Tennessee, where I earned All-American honors and my degree. As I graduated, I was offered a coaching job at the United States Military Academy at West Point. It was an honor and a privilege that I only fully appreciated with time. While coaching the men's and women's volleyball teams that year, I was surrounded by excellence. It was all about excellence and effort...in academics, sports, presentation, and preparation. The cadets had to believe in themselves in order to achieve to the extremely high standards required of them. Success, again I discovered at West Point, is powered by our thinking. As I coached these high-achievers, I noted that there were obvious times when they too needed occasional encouragement and a nudge to believe they could do it. This was especially evident when they were acquiring new skills and dealing with the unfamiliar. I found myself saying, "You can do it" constantly, both to them and to myself.

Without a positive mental attitude, a dream of accomplishment is unattainable. During my time at West Point, *You can do it* held a two-fold meaning for me. My desire to compete at higher levels in volleyball was keen; I had my sights set on playing for the U.S.A. Women's Team.

Since I hadn't received an invitation to the tryouts, I had to write several letters to request a tryout. I felt like I was repeating the effort I'd made to find a college. It took belief and persistence because I didn't receive any immediate response. So I solicited letters of recommendation from everyone who had coached me and knew my abilities. Once again, *I can* gave me power and hope, helping me believe that all things are possible. And bless West Point; what an ideal place to be while preparing to try out for the U.S. national team.

I received an invitation and went to the tryouts at the Olympic Training Center in Colorado Springs. I arrived with many girls from around the country. It was a most intimidating time for me, and I found myself mumbling *I can do this* as I walked through the entrance with my luggage in hand.

There were 64 girls invited. After the first day of physical testing, there were about 44 girls continuing. Four days later, only 18 of us remained. Only nine would be selected. Many coaches surrounded the court and evaluated every move we made. On the final day, they called us together to announce the results of the tryouts. Talk about tension in a room! I sat up front and, while we waited, I reviewed the dream I'd had ever since I saw Bruce Jenner win the decathlon at the 1972 Olympics.

They called out the name of the first girl to make the team...then the second...then the third and fourth and fifth and sixth. I slowly sank down in my chair and in my heart as the seventh and eighth names were announced. Then they called the ninth name. It was my name!

I couldn't comprehend the moment. I was so elated. It was wonderful to know that my efforts and belief in self had yielded extraordinary results. I bowed my head and reaffirmed my gratitude for the gifts and abilities I'd been given to perform at such a high level. Dreams really can come true. I MADE IT! So I thought.

In early 1985, I moved from West Point to the volleyball training site in San Diego. It was a bonus and a blessing. I never thought that I'd be living in California. We started training with our goal clearly and always before us...the gold medal in Seoul for 1988.

CHAPTER 3

I will.

As I began training with the U.S. national team, I soon discovered that I had to muster all my energies, attitude and more to perform to the high degree of excellence demanded of us every day. This elevated level of competition is not for the faint of heart or for those who don't sincerely believe they can do it.

This was when I realized I needed something to augment *I can*...to reinforce it with the purpose, drive and discipline necessary to compete at this world-class level of competition. I found it in the simple declaration: *I will.* I used it as a self-motivating tool for discipline and control, and the effects of this second affirmation kicked in immediately.

According to Webster's, *WILL* means *conscious choice*, and it also includes the meaning of having a *strong, fixed purpose*. Both meanings with all their implications were right-on for me. It seems to me that these two aspects of the will are best expressed in two ways... by goal-setting and by personal habits. Both have to do with intentional living. Together, they reflect taking responsibility for your development as an individual and accepting the responsibility to become your very best for the team. I see it as breaking old, bad habits and generating new, good habits to most effectively pursue your goals. I like to say: Dream big and do the ordinary with such consistency that your dreams become reality. When you affirm to yourself that *I can* and *I will*, you set your goal and your purpose to succeed, no matter what it takes within moral and ethical boundaries. Will power is the personal means to extraordinary accomplishment.

This second affirmation is something that came to me progressively, developed by my own life-experience. I think most people who know me or listen to me speak on stage perceive me as a strong, purposeful, decisive woman. This was not always the case.

About the time I entered junior high school, to enlarge my world beyond sports and school and to round out my interests, I was encouraged by my parents to learn to play a musical instrument. I chose the clarinet because my big sister, Carolyn, had taken up playing the clarinet the year before. While I liked it and worked at it, I have to admit that musical ability was not one of my gifts. I recognized that I played better with my feet than with my fingers. I may have been an all-star on the softball team, but I was a struggling beginner on the clarinet. There were moments of great self-doubt as I attempted to master the instrument to an acceptable level of beginner's competence.

I remember how nervous I was when it came time to play at a recital. I was way outside my comfort zone. Any instructors' evaluations from those recitals would have carried the comments: A for effort. Keep trying and believing.

I was never very confident in my skill, but I practiced, persevered, practiced more, and improved. I stayed with it and was in the band through the ninth grade. Graduating from junior high, I had to make a decision. Should I perform with the high school marching band as my sister was doing or should I give up the clarinet and compete in high school athletics? Even though it appears now to have been a very simple decision for me, at the time I really had to think about it and seek advice from my mom and dad. Should I continue and develop my abilities further on the clarinet, following in my sister's footsteps, or should I pursue my natural bent for sports where my ability and success had already been demonstrated? It seemed such a hard choice. Looking back, I realize that I made it hard for myself because I had not yet developed my own will.

I was having difficulty in deciding to go with what I found a joy or to live someone else's dream. It was a dilemma because I respected my sister greatly. Staying with the band would mean more time for us to share an experience in common and grow together. I came to the conclusion that I needed to do what I really loved doing...competing in sports, sweating, pushing myself, and working hard to help the team.

Up to the time I entered high school, Carolyn had always been a role model and we had a close connection. We were deeply involved in our church youth group. My sister and brother and I attended every week and were very much into activities within the church.

We went to youth camps every summer. At one such camp, in small groups, we were working through a workbook that dealt with heart matter. There was a question that asked, "If your house caught fire and you had a chance to grab ten things before getting out, list in priority what items you would take." The object was to teach us about priorities. A few years ago, I rediscovered my old, battered workbook and read my answers. I was shocked to see what I had written, and how it related to my dilemma in making the decision about athletics or marching band.

My first response was not family photos or my Bible, not clothing or food, not books or appliances; I wrote that I would grab my sister's clarinet and make sure it was safe. What in the world was I thinking when I wrote that?! However, it does illustrate my deep connection to my sister's influence.

Now that I look back, I recognize the impact of those years. Fortunately, I was forced to make choices to learn and grow and try. More fortunately, they were benign, formative choices, and fear was not a factor. They were the beginning of learning to take risks to succeed...which we all must do throughout our lives. Happily, they came at the early stage of learning valuable life-lessons.

What was the principle lesson I learned from this? That in order to achieve and find fulfillment and enjoyment in achieving, I had to step beyond the familiar and accept personal risk. I learned that disappointment and losing could be consequences; that even condemnation or ridicule were possibilities if my own choices did not coincide with someone else's expectations.

I regard the decision for athletics or band to be a defining moment in my life's direction. I could have sat on the sidewalk watching my cousins run; I could have moaned about having to do relay races and jumping events, about getting sweaty and fatigued during those week-long field days. I could have chosen my sister's path as opposed to following my own heart and natural abilities. But instead I decided to be a player, not a spectator in life. I made the right choice for me...to engage and compete and give my best. As far back as I can remember, I've had within me a great desire to do well. If I was going to do anything, I was going to give it my all. There has always been a passion in me to excel. I have always wanted to win.

I was brought up in a military family within a military environment. I've always been proud and happy about that, and it has contributed positively to my character. My military upbringing instilled in me a strong sense of discipline and duty. It also helped shape my self-reliance and sense of responsibility. My dad's dedication and military bearing were wonderful examples for his children; and the result was a secure, disciplined early life. The military opened the world for my mother. She saw a lot more of life and travel and varied society than she probably ever would have seen if she stayed close to her roots in Sumter, South Carolina.

The military gave us a controlled life based on commitment and fairness. It also gave us definite responsibilities: to be respectful, to do the right thing, to own up to our mistakes, to have a complete sense of honor and integrity. The military depends on developing trust and leadership. These qualities were drummed into us as our parents constantly emphasized them. We learned to respect the order and system that is in place; that there are superiors and subordinates; that we can always strive to be more, but with regard for existing authority; and that whatever we did, to do it completely and to the best of our abilities.

Every summer, the Thunderbirds performed an air show at the bases we lived on. It was a certainty that I would be one of the earliest there and one of the last to leave. Year to year at every show, I would stand in line to get their autographs. I was fascinated by their precision and inspired by their excellence. To me they exemplified the concept of TEAM...*Together Everyone Achieves More!*

I stand in equal awe today at the Blue Angels as they perform near our house in Southern California. When I recently met one Blue Angel pilot and talked with him at length, I was like a kid in a candy shop. It was a realization that childhood dreams can come true.

The core values of the military surely had an impact on my work ethic. I choose to do my work diligently. I choose to trust the systems to which I have made commitments. I admire trustworthy people and try to prove myself trustworthy. My passion for excellence has been fortified by the Thunderbirds and the Blue Angeles and my association with the military.

As we grew up, my parents chose not to make our decisions for us. They always sat us down at the dinner table and talked with us about the situation and the available options. And they always directed us to consider the consequences of our actions. Mom and Dad would say, "Remember, it's your decision. When you make it, stick with it and deal with the consequences." They wanted us to consider carefully, think clearly, and take responsibility for our actions.

As a result of all these factors...inner drive, upbringing, family values fused with military correctness...I've become the person I am today. And I am fortunate and happy and thankful for what I have achieved and for what I have to offer others. It is the grand consequence of all my actions and the product of my own will with a lot of prayer. That, more than anything, demonstrates for me the power of *I will*.

CHAPTER 4
I believe.

The first two affirmations, *I can* and *I will*, worked very well for me as I progressed in sports toward the Olympic team and in my daily life apart from athletics. However, at a certain stage during my training, I came to feel something was lacking from my affirmations...or, perhaps more correctly, I felt the need for something more, something beyond my own self-reliance and determination.

My affirmations only became complete when I added the declaration, *I believe*, which for me holds a special, life-completing meaning. The dictionary definition says *BELIEVE* means *to take as true or real*; secondarily, *to have confidence in something or someone*; and finally, *to have faith, especially religious faith*.

I take as true or real many things. I have confidence in myself and others. And I take issue with the sequencing of those meanings in Webster's. Belief in God should be placed first in tribute to the Divine Power that moves and motivates us all.

Yes, I have religious faith, and I have found that I needed it throughout my life to accomplish and achieve and endure. It is the final factor that has made me strong and complete. I wholeheartedly practice the faith in which I was brought up. The Bible is the bedrock for my convictions.

So for me, *I believe* has a significance far beyond simply believing that I can and will do what I set out to do. I believe that we are inspired and helped by God and that we have a responsibility to do our best to live up to that inspiration. I also get a sense of being assisted and directed by a Force beyond myself, and I desire that feeling.

From my earliest of days, my actions, thoughts and behaviors have been shaped by my faith. In the center of my soul, I know that each person has great value because each of us is created in the image of God. We are here by design and have each been given special gifts and abilities that are specific and complete within ourselves. Every one of us has been put on this earth to fulfill a destiny that no other person can fulfill. And even though we may not realize our true value and purpose, we must strive to find it in ourselves.

We have a great responsibility to love and help one another. My primary passion is to inspire people to believe in their God-given gifts, to believe in their inherent value, and to believe in themselves. When you have this perspective...despite anything that happens to you or affects you to the contrary...you grow in deep understanding, as I am sure I have. And you find your world an extraordinarily different place, as I did. You live an extraordinary life in the midst of the ordinary world. It changes your view of the world at large and it makes your private, personal world a better place. It happened for me.

As part of our church group activities when I was a preteen, I was in our youth choir. Some of my experiences from that time and that choir had a profound effect on me.

I joined the choir because my sister Carolyn and brother Jim had joined and it seemed like fun. Sound familiar? I was still a follower then, but it was part of the process of finding myself. Here again, even before enrolling, I knew that I had a so-so voice and limited ability, that my feet worked better than my mouth, but I was willing to try. My main reason for joining was the choir director. Enthusiasm, excellence, and enjoyment poured from every pore of her being. In retrospect, I recognize that I was so attracted to her because she exemplified what I wanted with all my heart and soul...to do with excellence and enjoy what I was gifted at. The majority of us were untalented, but she brought us together and made us shine like the morning sun. We performed for many churches and even did an Outreach program at a prison. I mention this because I was deeply moved by performing inside the walls of the prison. Actually, I was also terrified, but at the same time fortified because of the choir director's calming confidence. And I recognized that our prisoner audience probably needed encouragement in an entertaining form; we might be their only ray of sunshine that day.

It turned out to be a phenomenal experience, and it moved me so much that it was a direct influence on my decision for a major in college. I concentrated on Criminal Justice and earned a bachelors' degree in this field. For some unfathomable reason, one of the inmates decided to write me a three-page letter, and he gave it to me after the event. The heart of it communicated his struggles and desires. His struggles were about the hard life; his desires were to have a better life. I was so deeply moved by the letter that I couldn't find peace within my spirit for months. Why? I didn't know at the time, but now I see it as a directional signal for my own desires: to help others find the way to be their very best and to inspire hope in others despite their circumstances and environment.

Belief and hope are interconnected and dependent on each other. Both are vital to an individual's well-being and progress. I passionately want to affect those struggling with negative thinking and effect a positive change in their outlook.

CHAPTER 5

Family is my foundation.

Another of my strongest beliefs is in the power and goodness of family. I thank heaven that I have been blessed with my parents, brother, sisters, and upbringing; and that I am blessed with my husband and children. They are my joy and comfort and a constant source of strength and energy in my often hectic life.

It is a basic fact of construction that a house is only as strong as its foundation. Similarly, I am convinced, a person is only as strong as the material and the foundation she or he comes from. I am pleased to tell you that I am made of good stuff. I came from good, hard-working people who overcame the trials and tribulations of race and the deprivations and needs that went with it, who grew and made their way independently as this country grew in tolerance, acceptance and opportunity.

Begin with my parents who were my beginning. I think of them and cannot conceive of a better start in life or anyone better to be my parents than my mom and dad. They have been married for more than forty years, and they are a wonderful example of unconditional love. Theirs is a bond that is loyal and committed despite anything said, done or supposed. And it extends beyond themselves. They have always been there, a phone call away to help in any way. Because of the difficulties of their own childhood environments, my parents wanted us to have a better life.

For me, one of the most impressive things about my father, James Robinson, is his exemplary work ethic and dedication to duty. While I was growing up, I don't recall that he ever missed a day of work due to sickness, injury or attitude. One example of his commitment was the day he had four wisdom teeth pulled and went back to work in the afternoon.

My memory is of him leaving for work every day and being home for dinner with us every evening. In addition to his perfect record in the Air Force for 24 years, Dad only missed one day due to sickness in his 25-year career after the military. His rule was: "Whatever you do, give it everything you've got." He believed in leading by example, and there is no doubt he got this from his father.

Dad was born and raised in Pittsburgh, Pennsylvania. His father, Solomon, had been a sharecropper in South Carolina. The way it was told to me, my grandfather got into an argument with an overseer and it escalated into a physical altercation. Solomon jumped a freight train to escape a retaliation that probably would have killed him.

The freight train took him to Albany, New York, where he met and married my grandmother, Edna Knott, a domestic worker who was 25 to 30 years younger than he was. Solomon was 59 years old when my father was born. They had ten children; three were younger than my dad and six were older.

Because his father was an older man when Dad was born, my dad grew up in a much more subdued environment than he would have in a home with younger, energetic parents. Solomon was uneducated, and the family lived on the brink of poverty. Grandfather didn't talk a lot, hardly at all, but he was a hard worker and did his best to provide for the family. They never lacked for food, even though my grandfather's paycheck only came to $55 a week to feed the family of twelve. Despite their own circumstances, they never turned down a neighbor or a stranger who came to their home for help or a meal. My grandparents knew what it was to be needy, and I am proud to say that they were kind, charitable, sympathetic folks.

My quiet grandfather set an example by his actions, and that explains why my dad is much the same in his own manner. My father shared a story from his youth with me, and it brought home why Dad is the man he is. The family lived in a small, two-story house near the railroad tracks. Hobos hung out nearby all the time. Dad was walking home one day when a hobo came up to him. The hungry hobo asked Dad to go and get him some food and said he'd pay my dad a dime. That seemed big money to my father at that time.

Dad went home and told his mother about the incident. His mother, who always made enough spaghetti to feed one more, readily gave a huge plate to my dad to give to the hobo. My father found the hobo who ravenously ate the spaghetti and profusely thanked my dad. My dad asked for the promised dime. The penniless hobo made a show of looking for the dime and told my father he was sorry, he'd lost it. Dad walked home dejected with his head hanging and told his mother what had happened. She smiled at him and said, "That poor man never had any money, and it's not important. I want you always to treat people as equals. Don't ever look down at any person and always lend a helping hand. Give without any expectation to receive." That was my grandmother, and that was her message to my father...and over the years to me.

Dad has followed that instruction as fully and as well as any person I've ever known. This generous quality of character was especially important to him, perhaps because it came so generously from his mother. He evidenced it in many ways. Often, it was by helping others with handyman tasks in the neighborhood. He was very handy with a variety of skills, and I would say to him, "Dad, you're the best neighbor anyone could want." He was always helping to fix a car or repair an appliance, and I remember him distributing holiday gifts and food to those less fortunate...which he continues to do to this day.

The charity and giving he learned from both his mother and his taciturn father. The skills, learned from his father, came from showing up uninvited at Solomon's worksites to help out. His father taught him everything from basic plumbing and electrical work to car maintenance. The work was often hazardous, sometimes scary, and frequently frightening, but Dad insisted on coming to help, against his father's objections. When it got particularly hairy, his father would ask, "Can you do it?"

"Yes, I can."

"Okay then..."

My dad saw in his dad what can be achieved with motivation and desire for a greater purpose than self. Solomon's example sparked my dad to live such a life. His father never quit, never asked for a handout, never complained about his lot in life, and never argued with his wife in front of the children.

That kind of personal strength makes for exceptional living and fulfillment in spite of tough circumstances. It sets a high standard for old-fashioned fortitude and a wonderful example for children. The correct, positive perspective about yourself paves the way to fulfillment and impacts generations to come.

As children, we were strongly encouraged by my dad not to complain. His mother told her children, "Deal with what you've got." What they had was two bedrooms for ten children, a single commode in the cellar on the dirt floor, cold water, heat from a kitchen stove, and a lot of deprivation. Unable to buy toys, they made everything they played with. For entertainment they had each other and their friends. To me, the remarkable result of all this is that it made them strong and determined and achieving.

It's a far stretch to use an analogy from golf, but one does apply: Play the ball where it lies. How powerful that rule is when used as a philosophical instruction for living! "Deal with what you've got" has influenced me beyond measure. My brother and sisters and I were constantly involved in service effort, and I really enjoyed it in Candy Stripers, Girl Scouts, Brownies, babysitting clubs, and church outreaches.

In ninth grade, my father was told he couldn't get into or make it in the finest high school in his city. His advisor enrolled him in a trade school to become a cook. On his way to the trade school for his first day, he had to take a streetcar and make a transfer downtown. While waiting at the station for his transfer car, he made a decision that changed his life. He said to himself: 'This is not what I want to do; I don't want to be a cook.' So he turned around, got back on a streetcar for home, and took steps to enroll in the high school he'd been told was not for him.

My dad became a straight-A student in that school. However, when he was 16, my grandfather got very ill and couldn't work anymore. By this time, Solomon was about 75 years old. My dad and two of his brothers did what they could to help the family out. Ultimately, Dad left school and went into the military.

Regardless, his decision to change streetcars and go to the high school of his choice was one of the most important decisions of his life...and subsequently of mine. From that day on, he vowed that he would not let another person decide his destiny. He knew that he had the ability to do whatever he decided to do. This was a philosophy he infused in all of us through example and consistent reiteration. Dad considered it supremely important, and we all benefitted from his determined pursuit of the subject.

My mother, Julia Croskey Robinson, was of the same mind as my father, but came to it in her own way. She was brought up in Sumter, South Carolina in a rural environment where people had limited means, felt stuck and seldom left. Like my father, Mom was from a relatively large family of seven children. Her father, Cleveland Croskey, had a steady job working at a casket company, and they were better off than most. Unlike many in Sumter, they never went a day without food on the table. My mom's mother, Sally Hunter Croskey, also a domestic worker, served the family and any guest who came to dinner.

In her early teens, my mom knew that she wanted more in life. During school vacations almost every summer, her family could afford to send her to Brooklyn, New York to stay with her aunts and uncles. These visits opened her eyes to a bigger world.

Riding up north in the segregated section of the train one summer, her uncle told her to look out the window at all the apple trees in one particular location. While she looked, he told her the story of Johnny Appleseed. From that moment, she knew her life would be different. Her uncle's story was a turning point. I find it a charming coincidence that it happened while she was on her way to "The Big Apple" before it was known as "The Big Apple."

My mom was tall and beautiful, and her exposure to the enlarged world of New York put the idea in her head to attempt modeling. When she returned home, she shared her dreams and goals with her mother. My grandmother told her to go for it. Paralleling my father's philosophy, she advised Mom to make something significant of her life, never give into peer pressure, follow her passions, and strive for excellence.

My mom took her mother's words to heart, but her pursuit of a modeling career was voluntarily cut short. She met my dad when he was stationed at Shaw Air Force Base near her home, and that happily turned into the nurturing life for which she was destined. She never became a model, but she availed herself of all the opportunities that came her way. Choosing family first as her role, Mom stayed home to raise us. When we entered high school, she went to nursing school, then was a nurse for more than twenty years.

I have two sisters: Carolyn, who is one year older than I am, and Stacey, who is eleven years younger. My brother James died in January 1997 after the Atlanta Olympics, in which he carried the torch while representing the Georgia State Troopers. We grew up in a secure atmosphere as happy kids at a succession of military bases where my father was stationed. From our interactions with each other and our friends, we learned the social skills we'd need in later life: how to get along, respect for others, and how to occupy and entertain ourselves. We had good teachers, our own parents foremost among them. They taught us well, and, as I look back now, we turned out well.

Through vacation trips to South Carolina and Pennsylvania, we knew our uncles and aunts and cousins, and that gave us a feeling of belonging in an extended relationship. There were great times of family get-togethers, barbeques and dinners, games with cousins, and all the joyous childhood moments that come with being part of the larger family.

I was born in South Carolina in the same town where my mother was born and raised. We lived there for the first four years of my life, and we came back regularly to vacation at my maternal grandmother's house. I relish those times with their picnics, swimming, and sports. I cherish the moments I spent with aunts and uncles and cousins.

When I was eleven, something happened that showed me how wonderful my mother and father really were. At our Scott Air Force Base housing in Illinois one day, my mother received a telephone call from Sumter. My mother's older sister, Shirley, had died. What a sad day it was. We immediately loaded up the car and drove to Sumter. I vividly remember wishing I could ease my mother's grief and pain.

The funeral and surrounding events made me appreciate my parents' composed, caring strength. A short while after the funeral, Mom and her brothers and sisters met to discuss what to do about Shirley's six orphaned children.

After much discussion and prayer, my parents announced their decision to adopt her six-month-old infant daughter, Stacey Renee. To illustrate how kids think: I had just gotten a new puppy named Muffin, and now I was getting a new sister. I was thrilled!

Their unconditional love and complete acceptance of Stacey into our family affected me as nothing else has. I still reflect on their goodness and on their dedication to family. And I hope I would have the love and gumption to do what they did. It made a dramatic change in our household, but Mom and Dad kept us on-task with the regular responsibilities of daily living. By doing so, they demonstrated to us that stability is important. And they demonstrated the strength of heart that made it possible.

The entire episode was a learning experience for me. When the foundation and family are strong and supportive, storms and disasters can be survived by sheer consistence, persistence, love and commitment.

My parents continue to be a cornerstone of strength for the Sumter family, our family in Pittsburgh, and for all of us. They have endured much, and I love them for their steadiness, their selflessness, and for living to serve others. They have shown me what it means to be good parents in the highest meaning of family.

CHAPTER 6

My Irish blessing.

Brian Buffini came into my life while I was training with the U.S.A. volleyball team in San Diego. I was very active in my local church, and we first met while I was attending a Bible study class.

At the time, almost all of my energies were focused on volleyball. There was not much room in my life for anything except practicing my faith and volleyball. I was dedicated to becoming an Olympic-caliber athlete, and that required a great deal of sacrifice. My time was spent working out, training, traveling, resting, and replenishing myself by studying God's Word. That was my way and my world for three years from 1986 to 1988. It was almost monastic. This focus, I believe, helped me to become the player I dreamed of becoming.

Bible study was held regularly at the home of Brian's brother, John, whom I had come to know well through our church. Brian, who had recently immigrated to America from Ireland, lived with John early on. Usually near the end of our study classes, I often noticed him returning home late from his painting jobs. Because of John, I had already developed an interest in this Irish family from Dublin. I loved their brogue and, for some reason, I've always been attracted to the European culture.

I felt drawn to Brian. Strangely for me, I found myself wanting to know him better. Whenever he made an appearance, it seemed we'd end up chatting about things. Since I'm not much of a "things" person, I'd quickly direct the conversation to deeper, real life issues. We'd catch up with what was happening in each other's life. Our initial conversations were cordial and polite, but there was great energy between us; we could feel it; and we slowly began to build a true friendship. Looking back, we agree that we simply enjoyed being in each other's company.

The 1988 Seoul Olympics had come and gone, and I had completed my last national tour against the team from Japan. My commitment to the U.S. team was over, and I was free to come and go as I pleased. I had begun working for a mortgage company in La Jolla, a beautiful seaside village just north of San Diego. Brian was busy with his life, and I was making the adjustment from Bev, the volleyball player, to Beverly, the office professional person.

Our conversations and growing friendship were interrupted when I left the study at John's house to attend another home study group that met weekly. For a while, I lost contact with the Buffinis. Then, at one weekly meeting, as the study was beginning, who walked in but Brian! And I was more than glad to see him. Our renewed contact forged a stronger friendship. Whenever he attended that study class, I left a word of encouragement for him on his windshield. After one session just before Christmas, he walked me to my car and told me he'd like to get to know me better. That lit a little candle in my heart.

Brian was headed back to Ireland for the holidays, and I was headed home to Georgia. I wished him well and gave him my picture so he wouldn't forget me. That sounds romantic, but it was a volleyball shot.

Being home that Christmas was very special; it was a time for me to set new goals and a new direction for my life. While I was contemplating that and enjoying the time with my mom and dad, a card arrived in the mail from Ireland. It was from Brian. The message was simple and nice, but profound; I would even say life-changing for me; and, oh, by the way, I still have that card. It filled me with great joy and good feelings. Brian wanted us to get together when he got back.

The day before Christmas, I got a phone call from him in Ireland. I was overjoyed to hear his voice, and my heart was filled with love for him, though I didn't fully recognize it at the time. We only talked for a short while, but it still has a place in my heart as the call of a lifetime. The truth is that I melted when I heard his voice. The notion of having someone so interested in me and my warm reaction to it were new experiences for me. Until that call, I had kept myself an extremely private person, intent on my goals, and I hadn't permitted any distractions. Now I realized that I was free to allow our relationship to develop.

I returned to San Diego with great anticipation and determination. I went back to work and, just as I had done with volleyball, I became extremely focused to become an exceptional loan servicer. I worked hard at it and put in late hours.

One evening, as I was working after hours, Brian walked into my office. He'd been assigned to work at a site nearby, so he did a pop-by. That was the first of many pop-bys. It was a wonderful time for me. I lived and worked those few months to see him at the end of the day. I can testify first-hand that his pop-bys achieve extraordinary results.

Not only did he often drop in to brighten up my day, but he showed me that he cared and was thinking of me in other ways. On Valentines Day, all the ladies in the office received bouquets of flowers and visits or messages from husbands or loved ones. Brian didn't stop by the office, but he called to wish me a happy Valentines Day. His thoughtful phone call was enough to make the day for me. The next morning, I was sitting at my desk taking care of business when the receptionist came to me with a beautiful arrangement of red roses. Everything about them was sensational. They were luscious, and the aroma they gave off filled the entire office. The roses were so gorgeous that everyone stopped by my desk to check them out. Those beautiful flowers made their sender and me the subject of office gossip for days.

And he has never forgotten to show his love and caring. On our twelfth anniversary, he stunned me again when a florist arrived at our door with a van-load of roses. I presumed that the van was filled with orders for many others...until the driver returned again and again to our door. Brian had sent me twelve dozen roses. The house smelled like a flower shop. It was wonderful and caring and so like him.

We began to spend more time together. Our first night out was a real trip. I was nervous and anxious; I knew I had warm feelings for him, but I didn't know where it was leading. Brian knocked at my apartment door and escorted me to the parking area. The lot was so small that my tiny Yugo barely fit into the parking space. When we got there, I saw this long white limousine parked next to my car and sticking out into the street. Brian walked to it and ushered me in. I didn't say anything, but I was very impressed. My first limo ride ever! Brian had bartered his painting services for the limousine, and somehow that made it even more romantic for me.

We had a great evening. My feelings lived up to the song: "Heaven...I'm in heaven." Our relationship grew and got stronger, but I remained guarded in my consideration of where we were headed. We were going along well, having fun together attending sports and cultural events and visiting with friends.

One day, Brian phoned to tell me he was headed out of town for the weekend to the Grand Canyon with a friend of his who was also his mentor. I knew it would be a great time for him because the Grand Canyon is such a majestic, inspiring place. I thought about him all week and wanted to surprise him when he returned, so I went with his friend's wife to the airport to pick him up. When he got off the plane, he was wearing a cowboy hat and looked rough and rugged. I think my delight at seeing him was evident.

When I dropped him off at his apartment, he said, "Bev, we've got to talk. I had an extraordinary time, and I can't wait to take you to the Grand Canyon. While I was sitting on the edge of one of those most magnificent cliffs, I was smitten. At that moment in my heart, I realized that God has given me unconditional love for you. I know one day we'll be married."

I was stunned and deeply touched. I felt the same, but because I was so guarded and because this was a new experience for me, I simply replied, "Oh, that's nice." I smile now when I think of that moment. If he wasn't the confident man he is, my wooden response might have turned him away.

As we grew closer and it became obvious to everyone that we were courting, quite a few people registered concern because of our racial difference. That concern came from relatives as well as friends. When I told my mother on the phone that I was finally seeing someone, she said, "Oh, really?"

"Yes," I said and hesitated, "and he's from Ireland."

Long pause...

"Beverly, there aren't many black folks in Ireland."

"No, mom, not many. He's white."

Long silence...

In virtually every such instance, initial reaction turned into realistic acceptance. My folks often spoke with Brian during my frequent calls. They liked him and grew to like him more and more.

On an ideal night in August 1989, Brian took me out for a wonderful dinner and a beautiful sunset on the California coast. As we walked the boardwalk, he asked me to consider being his wife. Knowing me to be a cautious person, he gave me time to consider my response. By the time we got to the end of the boardwalk, it was dark and the stars were twinkling high above. We sat on the sea wall and listened to the surf. Suddenly, Brian dropped to his knees in the sand and proposed again with a song, *I Only Have Eyes for You*. It was so romantic, but I couldn't fully commit. Our evening ended, and I was left to consider this important life decision.

For Thanksgiving, we flew to Georgia so Brian could ask my mom and dad for my hand in marriage. It was important to both of us that our parents approve. His folks were in Ireland, so we called them, and they gave us their blessing. It was wonderfully comforting. My folks were not so easy. This was Brian's first face-to-face meeting with them.

Football on Thanksgiving Day made it almost impossible to communicate with my father. He loves football, and it was on every moment. Down with my dad went Brian to watch a game, then another game. In a lull, I could hear Brian begin, "Mr. Robinson, I'd like to..." and be drowned out by "TOUCHDOWN!"

By our last day in Georgia, Brian had become anxious to have his talk with my parents about us, and they did. I wasn't in the room, but I would have loved to have been a fly on the wall. They talked for quite a while, and my mom and dad voiced their serious concerns and reservations...but in the end they consented and gave us their blessing.

It's funny how everything happened over holidays. That Christmas back in San Diego, Brian was taking me to a concert. We were to meet his brothers to hear an Irish group downtown. When he came to pick me up at my apartment, he knelt and sang our song, *I Only Have Eyes for You.* Only this time, he finished by presenting me with an engagement ring. This time I was ready and ecstatically said Yes. That evening, we went with the Buffini brothers to celebrate this special occasion at the Chieftans performance. Appropriately, the music was Irish traditional.

We were married nine months later. I was warmly received into the family by his father George, mother Therese, sister Louise, and brothers, Dermot and Kevin, all of whom still lived in Ireland. Brian promised me that I'd never have a dull day with him. That promise has been more than fulfilled.

He began in real estate while I was still working at the mortgage company. We both worked hard, following the examples of our hard-working parents. On call constantly, Brian lived by his pager and was busy at work a great deal of the time. I had been raised in the military with a steady paycheck, so depending on inconsistent commissions was new to me.

We were typical of many young married couples, very busy and very scattered. We had the illusion of order and purpose, but in reality we were disorganized, sinking into debt, and floundering. His business was not going where he wanted, and our quality of life was unacceptable. We were both making a living, but we were short-changing ourselves as far as time together and truly meaningful pursuits.

Two years into our marriage, we had our first son, Anthony. Brian and I both welcomed children and were thankful for him. When it came time for me to return to work after maternity leave, I dutifully went back because I felt I had to. For six months, Brian or I drove Anthony to day care and picked him up from day care. We were fortunate because the lady who took care of him, Annie Taylor, was a good and responsible friend.

However, Brian decided one day, after taking Anthony to day care, that there had been too much day care for our son. Brian called me at work and told me he wanted me to give two weeks notice so I could stay home with Anthony. That's what I wanted, and Brian knew that. I appreciated his taking responsibility for action, but was somewhat fearful because my income was providing stability and insurance for our family. I wondered how we were going to make this work and how we'd make it without my paycheck.

It required faith...in God, Brian and myself. There are times in life when we are called upon to act and then work it out. This was one of those times. Brian describes it as: "Fire...Ready...Aim!" I gave my notice and stayed home to take care of Anthony. I was happy and thrilled to do so.

The shortcomings of our life grew more and more apparent to us until there came a day when Brian said, "We've got to make some changes here."

Brian meant it and called a "Time out!" on the game of life we had been playing. He reflected, he prayed and took the time to evaluate himself, our family aims, and his business. He considered everything carefully and came up with some life-changing goals that he wrote down to give them final validity. He shared these goals with me, and he shared his hopes and dreams for us. He identified our core values and built a vision for us as a family. It required a commitment to intentional living, and we made that commitment. It gave us direction and unified us in action. *I can, I will, I believe* became *We can, We will, We believe*. And our lives changed.

Not everything changed overnight. We frequently had our backs against the wall while we worked our way out of some deep holes. There were taxes due and bills to pay, and our time together was often out of balance with what we wanted. There were times when we felt we were chasing our tails or running like mice on a wire wheel. But, over time, we began to see positive changes. They came about because Brian had set clear goals and our core values were becoming more focused. We were spending more quality time together as a family; we were paying off our debts; and we were taking time to share our thoughts and hearts with one another.

Because Brian stayed strong in his resolve, I gained strength. Because we were committed to a better life, we not only grew ourselves but noticed those close to us impacted by our example. Amazing as it may sound, all of this happened because Brian took time out to rethink our approach to our lives. And wrote our goals down on paper. And generated the deep resolve to learn from our mistakes, to commit to intentional living, to change positively, and to move forward.

We continued to grow personally, financially, and in family. I had my hands full at home with Anthony and Anna. Brian's real estate business, innovatively based on clients solely by referral, was blossoming. He was making great strides by employing the concepts and principles he had developed during his time-out period, most of which were contrary to conventional real estate practices and thinking. I occasionally stopped by his office and helped when and where I could. It was exciting to be part of the enthusiasm and success.

Brian is a terrific communicator and negotiator, but so are many others. What made him surpassingly successful were his relational skills with people. In his business, he applied many of the principles he had formulated for us. His clients recognized his commitment and sincerity, the very qualities that attracted me to him. I heard from them the same things that resonate with me: "He really listens to us. He truly believes in me. He wants the best for me. He addresses our needs. He knew what was important to us. He follows through and gets it done. He's down-to-earth and genuine."

We grew together, and he built a highly successful real estate career. Success is attractive, and as Brian grew more successful, many opportunities opened up for him. Eventually he started to share his story with others through public speaking. The demand for him as a speaker grew, and he began traveling throughout the country.

He was away a lot, and I really didn't like being home alone. While I wanted him to share his story and achieve his dreams, I ached to have him home with me and our children. What made it doubly frustrating was Brian's genuine desire not to be away from home. He would much rather have been rolling on the floor and kicking the soccer ball around with the kids, and I knew that. It was a difficult time for me. I didn't discourage his speaking, and prayed for direction and to be supportive.

Knowing my feelings, he said me, "I want you to come and see what I'm doing." Well, I had seen and heard Brian speak, but not on the subject of business. I knew he had a great gift for it, so I knew he was doing it well.

I went, and it changed my perspective and my attitude. I was never prouder of him than I was in that room. It was absolutely electrifying. His passion and encouragement made it unlike any seminar I'd ever attended. I watched him share his story and principles for success with the audience. When I saw their responsiveness, heard their own stories of struggle and met the people individually, I realized that Brian was doing something vital and inspiring. It was much more than building a better business. In relating his story and telling them how he became successful, he was sharing his success and teaching them how to transform their own lives. In essence, he was describing how *I can* and *I will* could work for them and, through the strength of his own personality, leading them to *I believe*.

That day, I learned the fuller meaning of Providence and of Divine Providence. And Brian got more than my enthusiastic encouragement to continue his good work. From that point on, I wanted to be involved, to help.

Those speaking engagements and the travel I originally disliked became the nucleus for Providence Systems, which has become one of the leading personal and business coaching companies in the United States. It seems that my life is destined to be forever intertwined with coaching in one form or another, and I am happy with that.

While the success of Providence has been primarily the result of Brian's efforts and those of a dedicated staff, I'm very appreciative for the part I've been privileged to play in encouraging thousands of people in fulfilling their lives.

Brian says in Providence programs: Give, and you shall receive. It is so true. My life, our life, has been enriched a thousand times over in every way...by the people and the experiences and the self-fulfillment of helping others.

Even the inevitable mishaps, conflicts, problems, and minor failures take on a different twist when your mission is so high, human, and rewarding. We look back with affectionate humor at our modest beginnings, cramped quarters, early stumblings and hardships. We scarcely remember wondering where the next member would come from or writing a personal check to cover the pay-roll. We thank God for our survival and stability and success...and for the work we do. I believe it is what we were meant to do.

Brian carries his convictions over to his family. He is intent on helping the children and me be the best that we can be. He is my greatest advocate and champion, consistently challenging me to believe in myself as much as he believes in me.

His commitment to success and fulfillment in life are extraordinary, and Brian has been the catalyst to get me to the next level in many arenas. With him, there is no resting on past achievements or laurels. Often he reminds me that those gifts and abilities I demonstrated in team sports are still within me; nothing can take them from me. My own speaking endeavors and this book are results of his encouragement and support. He believes that my message of *I can, I will, I believe* will positive-ly influence many people.

Brian has been a constant source of strength and vitality for me as well as a source of great humor and laughter. One of our favorite funny moments was when I took him for laser surgery to have his vision corrected. He went in for the operation, and I sat anxiously in the waiting room filled with other patients and their escorts. Brian finally emerged without his glasses and wearing pin-hole goggles to shade his eyes. Every person in the room eyed him to see what they would look like after the procedure. As I moved to take his arm, he turned, stared at me, acted surprised, and said loudly, "Beverly, you're black!" We laughed and giggled about that all the way home.

Brian has steadfastly seen me for the person and the woman I am. Our love and appreciation of one another have grown greater each day. I marvel at what he has accomplished and at what we have achieved together.

There is a saying that is appropriate: *If you're fortunate enough to be Irish, you're fortunate enough.* But I would change that to fit my feelings for him: *If you are blessed by God to be Brian's wife, you are truly blessed.*

CHAPTER 7

Teaching and learning from my children.

Our children are our first focus. We have six; Anthony, Anna, Alex, Adam, and the twins, Amy and Alysha. They have come to be known as "The A Team" because their names all start with A; because we try to guide and teach them with love to be the best persons they can be; and because we coach them to depend on each other and us, as a team. Family closeness is so important and such a factor in a child's development that I believe it cannot be emphasized enough. When Brian and I got married, we wanted our home to be filled with children. He came from a family of six children, and I came from a family of four. We both knew the loving, reinforcing warmth of brothers and sisters and their importance to us.

After two years, we had Anthony. I remember focusing between contractions on the ultimate goal of this process. All those years of sprints and persistence and playing through pain paid off for a higher purpose on that November day in 1992. With Anthony came new expectations, dreams and hopes. He brought a new kind of joy into our lives, and a new responsibility. How would we handle it?

When it came time for formal education, we chose to home-school our children. We examined the options and weighed the pros and cons carefully. Brian and I discussed it at length with people and between ourselves.

We wanted to directly participate in their nurturing and shaping, not make them conforming. Home-schooling permitted us to have them together as a family and fully participate in their most formative years.

Our vision for our children and of our family guided us. We considered factors that included: transference of our family values, shaping our children's character, flexibility, academic excellence, and environment.

I teach them myself, and consequently I determine their courses of study and what they learn. That is an awesome responsibility, demanding and often hectic on a daily basis.

Home-schooling requires its own organization, disciplines, and guidance. It forces me to keep up with current curricula, methods and teaching techniques. It makes me measure the children's progress objectively, and sometimes takes all my stamina and resolve.

I see their attitudes, achievements and togetherness, and it is well worth any effort. They are responsive and responsible, secure, happy and bright.

Being our first child, Anthony was also our experimental model. He led the way for his brothers and sisters, and he did it most enjoyably. At the age of 11, he's into military history and has great interest in the Civil War and World Wars I and II. He reads constantly about military matters and attends many Living History events. If Anthony could pursue his military interests all day every day, he would.

Home-schooling not only grants him the time for this, it gives us a most effective way to use his interests to enhance other aspects of his education. I apply his military interests to activities for Math, English, Science, History and other study disciplines. Home-schooling affords this flexibility for independent study and individualized responsiveness.

There is never a dull moment, and not all my solutions or suggestions are gleefully or warmly received. I'm dealing with six different personalities daily, six strong-minded individuals. I genuinely try to remember and respect that. When they resist learning or rebel against the routine, I sometimes throw up my hands and cry out for help. And it goes both ways. If I'm having a bad day or reacting badly to their behavior, they pick up on that and are left with a bad taste and a bad example. The next best action for me to take is to ask for forgiveness.

Consistency and purpose are critical to the process. I often remind myself of our purpose in raising our children this way and teaching them at home: because we want them to be all that they can be.

It takes daily preparation and good habits for them and me. Being with them most of their day causes me to do a lot of soul-searching. If I'm running around like a chicken with my head cut off, that won't get it done. I have to stop and remember what's really important here: encouraging and helping them to be all that God has designed them to be. I continually seek the good and the potential that is in them.

Taking time and listening them are the keys. I'm a non-stop doer and a busy person; I've sometimes ignored or disregarded my own child's interruptive question because I was busy or in a hurry or preoccupied. That was a mistake on my part, more than a mistake because it's so taken to heart by the child.

I have to take the time to stop and look at my children. I've made it my duty to listen attentively and respond to their questions. I know I must acknowledge and encourage them. That builds their self-esteem. It communicates that they are loved, worthy and significant, and it means so much to them.

Remember to stop, look and listen to your children.

Our ways with our children are often immediately reflected back to us. I am encouraged and rewarded daily by the overwhelmingly positive things I see in my six children...and in all children. They are so optimistic by nature, open and curious and receptive, that they are a joy to teach and be with. Their development and growth is phenomenal as well as pleasing. It shows us we're on the right track in the way we're raising them.

We want to do more than give them a comprehensive education. We're trying to train them by principles, truth and habit to be upright, outstanding individuals.

Parenting is paramount with us, and it is intentional. We read extensively on the subject, attend seminars, listen to tapes constantly, and try to surround ourselves with others who are devoted to raising positive, industrious, godly children of great character.

Brian and I believe that we should be the primary influences in our children's lives. Therefore, we want to spend as much of their day with them as we can. We've learned over time that we should not relinquish the responsibility of providing loving guidance to our children and developing their core philosophies. We desire to give our children a strong foundation in scripture so that they may trust in the Lord.

The cornerstone of our child-rearing philosophy is Proverbs 22:6.

Train up a child in the way he should go,
Even when he is old he will not depart from it.

Although it is hard and we are all-too-human, we do the best we can to live up to these ideals. And we constantly seek to expand and reinforce the tools of development. For example, Brian and I strongly believe in the positive power of the motivational material we recommend through Providence to others; so we frequently play inspirational or instructive audio tapes on the sound system throughout the house. Naturally, our kids hear them while they go about their own activities. It has become so commonplace that they just do their own thing without seemingly being affected.

One of our most-played tapes is by the famous motivator, Jim Rohn, and on the tape he tells of the days when he was 25 years old with pennies in his pocket. He was "behind on his big-mouth promises to his wife and creditors were calling." Our entire family went to lunch with Jim, and he repeated the story for us, but left out the bit about creditors. In Jim Rohn's own manner of speaking, Anthony immediately inserted into the conversation: "...and creditors were calling."

And we thought he wasn't listening? Kids don't miss a trick! Brian is fond of saying, "Don't bother telling them what to do. They're too busy watching what you do." And, I might add, hearing what you hear, perhaps hearing it better than you do.

I have taught the children the power and purposeful significance of my own affirmations, and they have taken the words to heart. *I can, I will, I believe* have become important in their daily thinking, attitude, and talk. They constantly apply the affirmations to everything...from tedious tasks to what are for them earthshaking achievements. The end results of *I can, I will, I believe*, so earnestly applied, can be humorous sometimes, and can also be heart-wrenching.

Anna, our little gymnast, is a wonderful little girl. She is fun, nurturing, and always eager to help me. I consider her a special gift from God. Anna strives for excellence in all things and loves gymnastics. *I can, I will, I believe* are very much a part of her mindset. Brian and I discovered early in her young career how committed she was to the process. At her first gym, the coaches gave homework assignments in the form of physical exercises.

For one such assignment, Anna was to come home and practice doing her splits for five minutes each day.

Knowing her sense of responsibility, we left her alone to complete the assignment. A short while later, we came back into the room to see how she was doing. We found her stretched out on the floor, doing the splits, exhausted, with tears streaming down her cheeks.

"Anna, darling, what's wrong?" we asked.

"I hurt a lot, but I can't stop," she told us through her tears. "The coach said we have to go for at least five minutes on each side. I can and I will and I believe, but, Mommy, it hurts."

Then and there, we saw her extraordinary internal drive to achieve. While it is in large measure due to her God-given design, I credit it also to the many stories and illustrations we've read to her about perseverance and never giving up...and hopefully in some way to our example. And that kind of commitment has made her the California State Champion for her age group.

In other instances, the results have been warm and fuzzy and funny.

Our young son, Adam, is very independent and self-reliant. Often at age four when Adam dresses himself, he gets hung up with an article of clothing and I go to assist him. Usually, he resists my help and says, "Mommy, *I can, I will, I believe.*"

One day I was having a particularly tough time. Something in the house broke; the kids got muddy just before we were scheduled to get into the car; the baby twins were both pooping at the same time; and I was late for our appointment. Adam saw my state of mind and came to me. As I leaned down to speak with him, he cupped my face in his hands...as we sometimes hold our children's faces...and said, "Mommy, repeat after me... *I can, I will, I believe.*"

With the realization that I was getting a taste of my own medicine, I mumbled the affirmations by rote while staring down at the floor. Then he said what I sometimes say to him, "Now say it like you mean it!"

That was a wake-up call...an instant shot of renewed hope in my day. I was encouraged right away by Adam's strong conviction in what he was saying. It inspired me to change my attitude.

One afternoon, I heard strange thinking noises and, above them, the sound of five-year-old Alex declaring tremulously, "*I can...I will...I believe...*" over and over with obvious effort. I ran to see what he was doing and discovered that he was engaged in a mock sword battle with Anthony. Outmanned, outweighed and obviously overmatched, little Alex was resolutely doing his best to stay up with his older brother. I wasn't happy about the makeshift swords and the combat, but I was delighted at his determination and courage.

The children are so eager to help that occasionally I forget their size and limitations. Once, while I was busy with one of the twins, I unthinkingly asked Alex to help his little sister, Amy, out of her crib in the next room. Alex obediently ran to do it. Realizing immediately that she was too big for Alex to lift, I dashed into the next room. There was Alex, carefully maneuvering and lifting Amy from the crib, while repeating the entire time: "I can...I will...I believe." That was a mother's moment, one to cherish forever.

Lord only knows what lessons lie ahead from our twins, Amy and Alysha.

In this unconventional, lengthy process of raising and educating our children, many, many times I've said to myself, *"I can, I will, I believe."* These affirmations have helped me get through difficulty and self-doubt. I've learned that you do not teach your children; that they learn from you and through you. I believe that successfully raising children is all about giving. Giving all of me. Giving all my energy at this moment. Giving my total attention. Can there be a better return for giving of yourself?

CHAPTER 8
Learning from competition.

I've heard it said that sport builds character. Looking back over my life, I can see the tremendous effect it has had on me. My life now, my values and approaches and drive, have been indelibly shaped by athletics and competition. I now understand why I had such a passion for athletic competition: it challenged me. It gave me attainable goals, channeled my energies, and imposed the disciplines and rules I needed. It taught me the value of teamwork, hard work, sportsmanship, and fair play. Most importantly, competitive sports provided the arena for me to realize and utilize my God-given abilities and to grow as a person.

As far back as I can remember, I've had a great desire to do more than merely participate. I've always wanted to fully engage and win...to succeed. I started by playing a team sport, softball. That taught me the concept of teamwork at an early age, that I had to take responsibility and do my part. It also gave me valuable lessons in sportsmanship, selflessness, and dealing with personal disappointment.

In junior high school, our team went to the state playoffs. I played hard and well. To my eighth-grade thinking, I should have been named Most Valuable Player, but was not. I was disappointed and hurt, and I let it show. Tears rolled down my cheeks after the awards ceremony.

My father comforted me with words that I have ever since kept in mind: "Beverly, it's not about being named the best. It's about giving your best. Always remember it's the team that's most important. Be the best that you can be and trust God with the results. In your life, you'll have to face disappointments and unjust situations. Deal with what you've got, and do it with a happy, understanding heart. Believe in yourself and in your own value. Don't let the judgments of others affect your belief in yourself or keep you from performing your best."

His wise words have proved wonderful advice. They prepared me for later challenges, failures and successes throughout my college years, athletic and business careers, and family life.

As I made progress in local athletics, I gained confidence in my abilities and an appreciation for the gifts that God had granted me. I started looking for ways and opportunities to get to the next level. A flyer to one of my high school coaches advertised an all-sports camp at Auburn University in Alabama. Every athlete at my high school was made aware of this offer. I went to talk to the coach about it and learned later I was the only one who did. We found a way to pay the week-long camp fee, and I was off to the races.

It was a phenomenal experience for me. There were girls from all around the state of Alabama. I was the only representative from my city. It was a week filled with skills development in basketball, track and volleyball. Coaches from various state colleges came to conduct clinics and to watch us. That week and that experience built my confidence. I knew I had learned a lot and performed well.

On the final day, my self-appraisal was validated. I was named Most Valuable Player of the entire camp. By this time, I had matured enough to understand the true meaning of the award. It was not for outshining the rest; it was an acknowledgement that I had done my best.

It was also the first time that I recognized the importance of great coaching. As I followed their system and improved my skills so much in that one week, I realized it could lead to greater things. If I worked on it and practiced those skills diligently throughout the summer, and if I shared what I had learned and set an example for my teammates, we could all get to the next level, the state championships. As it turned out, we did well, but not well enough. The summer before my senior year, I attended volleyball camp. Coaches were there representing colleges from around the country. At the end of the camp, I was again named MVP.

Recruiting time was coming up for colleges. I was encouraged to write letters seeking an athletic scholarship for volleyball. A few schools showed interest in me. One, the University of Alabama, wrote back and offered me a full scholarship. What a boost it is when people believe in you! I went to Alabama and did very well. Even though the volleyball program was discontinued after my second year, it was a great experience for me.

I could have thrown in the towel at that point, but I didn't. I had so much more to achieve. I couldn't quit on my dreams. I knew there had to be a way to realize them.

Once again, I put myself through the difficult, dogged task of searching and writing letters to ask if any school wanted me. One did, the University of Tennessee. I was granted a full ride there, too.

Tennessee was nationally known for their women's basketball and track programs. I entered the land of peak performers. Once there, my world got bigger and my goals more challenging. Expectations were higher from coaches and teammates. I really began to understand the demands of excellence. If I wanted to be the absolute best I could be at this sport of volleyball, I had to expect the best from myself and those I counted on. I had to optimize skills and trust the new systems. I worked hard and believed, and it worked wonderfully well for me. As a result, I was named to the All-American Volleyball Team.

The turmoil and setback at Alabama turned out to be the best thing that could have happened to me. That experience and subsequent setbacks in my life have proven to me the truth of the axiom: *As one door closes, another opens.* And I have learned never, ever to give up...not on myself or my dreams.

As my senior year at Tennessee was ending, the U.S. women's v-ball team was playing in the finals at the 1984 Olympics in Los Angeles. I was watching on television because I'm a big fan of the Olympic Games; they represent a striving for excellence that I find inspiring. I was so inspired as a young girl viewing Bruce Jenner in the 1976 decathlon that I dreamed of being in the Olympics myself some day. I didn't know how or when or where, or even in what sport, but the thought of competing at such a high level thrilled me. While I watched the women compete and win the silver medal, I thought to myself: *I want to do this. I can do this, and I will do it. This is my dream.* The goal was set, and my direction was clear.

Instead of going to graduate school, I took the job as assistant coach at West Point, the United States Military

Academy. Here again was the opportunity of a lifetime. It sent rockets off in my brain. West Point was further entry into the world of peak performers. It engaged and enlarged my concept of excellence, and it provided the perfect training ground for Olympic preparation. I coached and trained at the same time.

The tryouts for the U.S. National Volleyball Team were held in Colorado Springs in February, 1985. Mine was the last name called for the team. Again, rockets went off within me. I was on my way to achieving my dream.

When I moved to San Diego to train, I learned that staying on the team required a continuing commitment to self and team every single day. Those who understood that and put out the effort survived and benefitted. Those who came in with a half-hearted attitude or with another agenda didn't last long.

Athletic competition at this world-class level is supremely demanding of time, energy, and concentration. There is no tolerance for mediocrity. Great things are expected of you each and every moment.

Staying on the team came at a high price with great sacrifice daily. My life was no longer my own. I learned to live every moment purposefully, to relish the routine and repetition, and to overlook the discomforts.

It was at this point that the concept of *Expect great things to occur today* came to me. As I willed my attention toward positive goals and results, it gave me an increase in attitude and incentive to succeed. It helped create positive energy and excitement to meet the challenges. At times when I lost focus, it helped me recall my purpose and refocus to work toward my goals.

I was convinced that intentionally committing to these ordinary daily tasks with great consistency would pay off in extraordinary results. I had to live to expect great things. Being there required me to daily face my greatest fear, failure. Belief in myself and my abilities was essential. That's why I'm such a keen proponent of surrounding myself with things that motivate and inspire: friends, tapes, books, whatever helps me to be my best.

Every day seemed the same. We worked on some aspect of the same skills over and over...with the same people at the same gym with the same volleyballs. My teammates and I endured the same schedule of workouts, strategy and study sessions, meals, and lights-out with hardly any free time. We slept and dressed out of suitcases, wore the same uniforms, and sweated the same every day...with floor burns and a twisted ankle here and there. The saving thought through all of this was its glorious purpose.

My goal was to play for the United States in the upcoming Olympics. The slogan was "Go for the Gold in Seoul." It was to prove a long, arduous process for three years.

Making the training team and traveling squad was no assurance of making the Olympic team. There were many more experienced and better-known players than I. We began with nine players, and I knew the size of the training squad would increase to fifteen or twenty with the addition of established players later in the process. I had to find ways to be a valuable asset to the team and to contribute so that I made a difference. It was all about developing and improving, trusting the systems and the coaches, and becoming an exceptional, invaluable player.

There were days when everything clicked for me, and there were days when not a whole lot went well. That left room for discouragement and doubt. Improper state of mind was the major reason for my bad practice days or for sub-par games in actual competition. When I analyzed the situation, I usually concluded that I lacked the proper mental preparation...attitude, positive thinking, game-plan preparation, or confidence. There were times when I found myself pressing so much that I was trying too hard and made mistakes. When I overtried, I got tight and tended not to think well or perform efficiently.

Our coach taught us...and I learned...to relax in critical situations and let it happen. When I was in control and relaxed and confident, my skills and play were consistently high. On this national team and on my college teams and at West Point, mental preparation was an important factor in our training. We were continually directed to visualize our moves in our minds. The image of success formed by visualization led to heightened performance with great confidence, efficiency and aggressiveness. It is easy to overlook what you have been taught. For me, it was a case of bringing into play something I already knew.

Great players want the ball and the responsibility at crucial moments. If you've ever played volleyball or any team sport, you know there are constant opportunities to make the play. Conversely, there are as many opportunities to screw up. At times early in my career, I allowed myself to be affected by the fear of making a mistake or error. My mindset was: "I hope I don't make a mistake.." or "I hope they don't serve this ball to me.." That kind of thinking was in itself a great mistake. When I thought like that, I usually played it safe and didn't take chances. In those instances, I lacked the aggressiveness necessary for winning play. It resulted in missed opportunities, possible loss, and quick substitution.

I learned quickly that there was no room for that type of thinking on the national team. We were expected to rise to every challenge. I came to welcome every opportunity that came my way as a chance to make a difference. I came to realize that achievement and success in volleyball, and in all sports and in life, depends on the absolute attitude of *I can*.

Competing is welcoming opportunities and challenges. Winning depends on fearless execution. For me, it was a learning process gained from the bad days and the bad plays. For a while, my mistakes and errors outweighed my successes. In volleyball, there are ample opportunities to be slightly off-target. Our coaches were always on us to shake off our mistakes and be ready for the next opportunity, the next play, the next ball.

Our head coach, Terry Lischevych, built us up or put us in our place as the situation dictated. He reminded us what an honor it was to be on the team; that there was a better chance of anyone becoming a brain surgeon than making an Olympic squad; that no one on this team was indispensable. We were constantly warned not to get complacent about our performance.

Almost weekly, it seemed, we saw new faces coming in to try out for the team. Those who came and went far outnumbered those who stayed. It was so competitive and stressful that my constant worry was whether I'd be there tomorrow. I was considered marginal, on the bubble in the 12th to15th slot, even though I was going all out to win a spot on the traveling team. Only 12 players got the opportunity to travel and compete throughout the country and the world, so I was forced to give it my all every day.

At our San Diego training site, practice was held daily Monday through Friday from 8:00 AM to12:30. Then we underwent a torturous afternoon program of conditioning which consisted of running, weight training, swimming, ply metrics, or other strenuous calisthenics. The focus was always on improving. Our coach regularly called us in for one-on-one meetings to assess our performance.

If we weren't in the gym training, we were touring and playing teams of other nations, and that involved national and international travel. I'm fortunate to have visited many exotic places this way: Russia, Cuba, Japan, Korea, Canada, and the Dominican Republic. I've been to China and visited the Great Wall and the Forbidden City.

A week before each trip, we were notified if we'd been selected to travel. Our first tour was on the West Coast against Korea. Talk about excitement! To put on the uniform and represent the United States was an unbelievably thrilling and honoring moment for me. Whenever my name was called, I was thrilled. And I felt bad for the other women who had worked hard but had to remain. Because I wanted it so much, it was devastating when I didn't make a road trip, especially when I was performing well and thought I should go. On those occasions, it was tough to go into the gym the next day and train without the entire team.

How did I handle those times? I bit my lip and trusted our coaches and their evaluations, but that didn't necessarily reflect my inner feelings. I found solace in my faith and in my favorite scriptures: "I can do all things through Christ, who strengthens me," and the text that says: "Whatever you do, do it with all your heart." That is ultimately where I found the strength to persevere; how I pushed myself when no one was there.

In the second year, I was picked to go on a trip throughout Western Europe. I was ecstatic. Shortly before we were scheduled to leave, I suffered a severe back injury. I was immensely frustrated at being left behind.

However, that injury and my exclusions from the traveling squad taught me fortitude. I learned to think differently about the seasons of life. I discovered that the seasons of life could change from month to month, and I needed to adjust my thinking. Trials and tribulations come and go; opportunities arise, and many pass us by.

I learned patience and endurance...to handle things beyond my control simply by waiting them out. I did the things I knew to do and trusted God for the final result. I did everything our coaches asked. Like a farmer who plows his field, sows the seed, fertilizes and cultivates, then waits...all the while I knew that in the final analysis I was dependent on forces outside myself. If I didn't learn from my setbacks, I was doomed to fall short or fail.

From the setbacks and injuries, anticipation and anxieties, through the more than three years that this process ruled my life, I learned finally and forever that the way to succeed is to endure and believe. It truly taught me to believe in what I brought to the table, in the coaches, in my teammates, in the system, and in God, who helps when all else seems to fail. Each obstacle and setback presented a choice for me to make...be negative and permit myself to sink low or fight pain and frustration and diligently work myself through it.

Three years and more came abruptly to a decision point one month before the Olympics. I found myself sitting outside the head coach's office with two other girls, Cathy and

Sherri. We were there to find out if we had made the twelve-woman team. Sherri went in first and came out in tears. After Cathy came out very upset, it was my turn with the coach. I sat down in the chair directly in front of his desk. My heart and anxieties were racing. I knew I was playing well and had an excellent chance. My hopes and dreams hung in the balance.

Terry, the coach, started talking. I could tell by the tone of his voice that it would not be what I wanted to hear. He said it was one of the toughest decisions he'd ever had to make, but they had selected someone else as the twelfth player. Sherri and Cathy and I would be alternates. We would travel to Seoul with the team and work out at practices, but we would not dress for the Olympic matches. It was a devastating blow to my mind and heart.

I was hurt viscerally and disoriented by disappointment. How was I going to tell my parents and friends? What about all the work and sacrifice that I had put in for almost four years. My mind was whirling as I left Terry's office. I had been rejected; I wasn't good enough to make it. My dreams and hopes were shattered, or so I thought. What to do next? My thinking was jumbled. My self-esteem was sunk...to the bottom of the ocean at that moment. Against my nature, and against my father's far-seeing advice when I was in the eighth grade, I let myself be deeply affected by a decision made by others about my performance.

I decided I was not in any shape to go to that day's practice and ended up calling Cathy. We both needed comfort and met with Bibles in hand. We read and we prayed and we cried. There was only God to turn to. I did some real soul-searching.

The following day, we went back to practice. Even though I didn't totally know why at the time, I knew what I had to do. I had to go back into that gym and expect great things; my responsibilities to the team and myself hadn't changed because my role had changed. I was the same person who had given her all and dedicated herself for years. My value was in knowing I had truly given my best; not in anyone else's opinion of me.

Faith to keep going was needed now. *I believe* was never more necessary. Please, God, give me the fortitude to face the hurt, the strength to believe despite the disappointment, the courage to continue to compete when hopes and dreams grow dim. It was a season of intense learning and trusting.

We went to the Seoul Olympics. I sat behind the team to watch them compete, but it was wonderful. To this day, that experience remains a highlight in my life. It was all about excellence, the thrill of victory and the agony of defeat. I am a better person for it.

The year before at our team banquet, I was greatly surprised to receive the Coaches' Award. While the recognition was gratifying, the true treasure for me was the entire experience. The real reward was what I learned from it.

CHAPTER 9

Lessons from life.

To most observers, my life now probably seems idyllic. I'm married to a very successful man and have a great family, nice home, fulfilling career, and all the comforts and trappings of success. But, like most of you, I still have to deal with life's darker events and moments of disarrangement, disappointment, disaster and despair. Life comes at me daily, as it comes at all of us, with everything from annoying petty problems to severe tests of our will, character, and faith.

Most turn out to be minor challenges, things to be handled with humor, a cool head or a good heart. My children are arguing; my car or an appliance goes bad; something I forgot to do suddenly creates a crisis; I'm late for an appointment. These things always seem to happen at the worst possible moment, and they happen to me, too.

For example, during the most demanding and critical days of finalizing this book to meet the printing deadline, a pipe burst upstairs in our home. The water flooded the house and ruined our brand new carpeting. The kids reacted riotously as we sloshed through the damage. Everything was a mess, including me. I had to get in plumbers and carpet people and put everything else aside. I said to myself *I can, I will, I believe* many times that day and over the next few days. Somehow, it all came under control, and I got through it. Someday, in the future, I'm sure we'll laugh about it. Sometimes God displays a strange sense of humor and tests us in funny ways.

Disastrous events in our lives are not funny, and they are difficult to deal with. Our own dark moments affect each of us grievously. One of the worst for me was the death of my brother.

Jim was a year younger than I. We hung out with a lot of the same people in our youth groups. As we grew into our teens, I gravitated to athletics and he chose different areas of interest. He was good-natured and a prankster who enjoyed being with his friends.

I was tall for my age, and Jim had always been shorter, so I had the upper hand physically. Just before my senior year in high school, we were horsing around, wrestling on the den floor. He pinned me down and made me scream "Uncle!" I hadn't really noticed until then that he had shot up seven inches in one summer. Suddenly my little brother was taller and stronger than I was. We relocated to Georgia, where Jim completed his final year of high school. I was off to college, and he was learning a new city and making new friends. After his graduation, he worked locally for a while, then decided to join the Air Force like his dad.

After his stint in the Air Force, he made the decision to become a Georgia State Trooper. When I heard that, I was thrilled for him. He had grown up and was taking on serious responsibility, and he had always liked helping people. He graduated from the state police academy and became a Georgia State Trooper. I was proud and happy for him. Whenever we talked or I saw him during visits home, he appeared to be doing well. And it struck me how perfectly his uniform fit his maturity and authority.

On a Friday afternoon in mid-January 1997, I received a startling call from my mother. She screamed into the phone: "Bev, your brother is dead! Jim's gone, he's dead! He's been shot, and he's gone!" I couldn't believe it. My brother was gone? It couldn't be possible. I felt myself sinking and began to sob, fought for control and told Mom I'd get the first flight home. Brian was traveling a lot at this time and was on the road at a Providence seminar.

Distraught and hurting, I called up our pastor. Then I called a wonderful, godly friend for more encouragement, consolation and hope, and she didn't let me down. She told me of a book, *Trusting God, When Life*

Hurts, that dealt with loss. I went and got it and read it during my flight to Georgia. I feel that God provided it as a support for me while I went through this devastating time. I read that book from cover to cover on the flight and soaked the pages with tears as I thought about my brother and shared the pain my parents must be going through.

My brother was honored and put to rest. The funeral was a beautiful tribute to him. The procession extended for miles and included a motorcade of police cars, public service vehicles, and a full complement of police, state troopers, and friends.

Those were some of the saddest and most devastating days of my life. From that wrenching week, I learned that tragedy brings focus. The death of a loved one reaches deep into the soul and provides great opportunity for self-examination and transparency.

The loss of Jim hit close to home; it was the only time I had to face a death in my immediate family, and the impact on me was enormous. It made me realize all the more how much our family and friends mean to us and how suddenly any of us can be gone. It reinforced to me that everyone has to go through times like this, and we should be compassionate, loving and understanding to one another because we are all joined by tragedy and triumph in common. It solidified my resolve to listen, understand and help others.

I saw that times like these bring out the best in people as they seek to console others, perform wonderfully kind acts, and react with sincere sympathy and consideration. I realized that much good and understanding and caring results from tragedy. I thought of Aunt Shirley's untimely passing and my parents' exemplary reaction; how it brought us my sister Stacey and showed me true compassion, caring and love.

It made me realize anew how trivial and temporary our daily problems are in comparison. And it helped prepare me to handle the large tragedies that might occur in my own life. I lived through it and watched my mom and dad, and I saw that we can endure anything if we have inner strength and faith in God's design.

Loss teaches us to make the most of our own time on earth; to live life to the fullest; not to procrastinate; and not to put off our goals and hopes and dreams. To this day, my mother constantly reminds me not to put off what I should or want to be about.

I loved my brother and often think of what it would be like if he were here. God has given me time to heal. My memories of Jim are cherished thoughts, and I will always treasure the times we had. I still hurt for my parents. At times, I see the loss in their eyes, and pain that time can't erase. They have found great solace in their faith, as have I.

Dire times are an inevitable part of life. Rain is as necessary as sunshine. For all its unique satisfaction and value to me, my own Olympic experience carried with it the element of great personal disappointment. And it gave me a moment I'll never forget...something to remember in difficult days.

I traveled to the Soviet Union in 1987 with the U.S. team. My most vivid memory of that trip is of when we were leaving the country. It was overcast the entire time we were in Russia. We hadn't seen sunshine while we were there. It was depressing. As we were flying out, we broke through the thick layers of clouds and soared into a bright, sunny sky. That moment illustrated perfectly to me the need for faith in troubled times. The darkness may seem so overwhelming, so full of despair, that we don't know where our help will come from. It is a trial. We must struggle against despair and find our way through the darkness. God will eventually give us the light to see our way, to provide perspective and resolution.

That passage from clouds to light illustrated for me that God is working in hard times for my good, even when I see no apparent reason or benefit. There are times when I need to quiet my soul and trust in God; know that I am part of something much greater; and trust that all is under the control of a trustworthy Higher Power than myself.

As for the rest...the minor, annoying occurrences and the more important problems that confront us in daily life...*I can, I will, I believe* help me handle just about anything. These affirmations have become my foothold and help me stabilize myself. They give me a starting point for positive action and prompt me to generate momentum.

It is my experience that momentum is critical to success in anything. As you get going and keep going, you gain energy, power and force. In team competition, I've been in many matches where momentum made the difference between winning and losing. If the team got off to a great start, we had the momentum and the advantage. If we made an error, departed from the game plan, or got over-excited, the momentum could suddenly shift to our opponents. The effect was amazing: loss of momentum affects not just the individual, but the entire team; it creates doubt, destroys confidence, breeds mistakes, and prevents winning and success.

The same is true in business. I have seen Providence Systems and Brian gain in success because they have kept the momentum going. It depends on believing and achieving, and it all begins in the mind. Confidence keeps it going and keeps us moving forward, overcoming obstacles and meeting our goals.

CHAPTER 10

It's all about people and helping each other.

People are important; things are not. Our achievements and the material things we acquire turn out to be relatively unimportant as we progress through life. How often have we seen and heard our seniors demonstrate that by their actions or comments?

"I have everything a person could want, but I wish I had my loved one back."

"It's only a car. Don't worry about it. Was anyone hurt?"

People are the irreplaceable elements of life. They are the true matrix we operate within, and they are what we truly relate to. Each person is vital to the whole cloth of mankind created by God. Every person is deserving of our consideration and caring and assistance.

"Love one another for My sake" says it better than I ever could.

As I look back, every achievement in my life, every step in my journey, is the result of help and encouragement from others. Everything I have or have done came from others in different forms of caring, nurturing, teaching, coaching, encouragement and love. Many have helped shape me by example.

At the University of Tennessee, I was privileged to room with Joetta Clark, the great runner who has since competed in four Olympics. She got up early every morning to run and never missed a day, despite rain, sleet, snow or ice. Every day she downed a tablespoon of foul-tasting cod liver oil because of its health benefits. Yuk!

I knew that Joetta was exceptional...that I was in the company of someone great. She displayed incredible discipline and was extremely focused on her daily objectives. In track and field, degree of training dictates readiness for competition; performance is truly a direct result of the time and effort put into training. I marveled at her discipline, determination and intensity.

Many of the outstanding athletes in the Tennessee program worked hard at their events. Off-court and off the track, they all went through the same kind of academic and personal struggles that I did. We all sought to find balance with our time and acceptance in our particular groups and relationships. Apart from sports, there were other distracting demands as we worked out daily and went for our athletic dreams.

Success depended on developing an iron-clad work ethic. Practices were to a strict schedule, so when it was that time, I was committed to practice. When I wasn't in the gym or the conditioning room, I had to somehow fulfill my other obligations. The effectiveness was in planning and not just letting life happen. Excellence doesn't create itself; it is achieved with intention and attention. Joetta Clark taught me all that by her example. She occupies a place of high regard in my admiring memory.

As an example of excellence, Edgar, the Providence company pilot, ranks high with me. He is recognized and respected in the Lear-jet community of private pilots for his exceptional professionalism and thorough mastery of all the details of flying. He constantly educates himself concerning new developments in flight equipment, techniques and safety.

He goes beyond professionalism by always providing superb service and great personal regard for his passengers. His every act and communication is faultless, and he performs his responsibilities with enthusiasm and respect.

I find his focus, conscientiousness and care inspiring. When I fly with Edgar, I know I am in excellent hands, and I am reassured and comforted.

People are the concern at Providence Systems. Over 200 individuals, personal coaches and staff, work with thousands of Providence members to improve their businesses and business practices, to make them all they can be, and to aid them in bettering their lives. Helping people is what we do, and I am honored to play a part.

Through appearing with Brian and speaking at *Turning Point Retreats, Peak Performer* and *MasterMind Summit* events, I have had the opportunities to reach thousands of people with my story and personally meet hundreds and hundreds who seek help with their lives. It is my mission and my dream to inspire them to positive action and to respond to every individual who seeks my help, guidance or advice.

Many relate to my own struggles, disappointments and failings. Many more see in my story a hope and methodology to overcome their own adversity and to get the best out of themselves through determination, attitude, and faith. Every one has their own story, result, and response.

A leap of faith. A client sent me a letter, wanting to share her renewal of confidence from a small personal triumph during our Peak Performer conference in Hawaii. She and her young daughter were enjoying the beautiful surroundings and warm water of the Grand Wailea resort. Her daughter insisted on going down a very high slide into the pool. Mom hesitantly and fearfully accompanied her daughter to the top of THE BIG SLIDE and awaited their turn. With great apprehension, mom walked to the edge. Her fear registered with the daughter, who looked up into the mother's eyes, grabbed her hand, and said,

"Mommy, say '*I can, I will, I believe.*' " Mom made the affirmations, gained courage, and went down the slide. From that singular experience, she felt renewed in confidence and consequently enjoyed some truly special moments with her daughter.

It took commitment and believing. When we take a step of faith, we move forward in our thinking. There's no telling how far we can go and what joys we may experience.

Brotherly encouragement. Another mother who was one of our ClubNet members was driving her sons to a baseball game. On the way, they were listening to tapes and talking about the affirmations. When they got to the game, little brother sat in the bleachers with mom as they cheered for big brother's team. When big brother came to bat, there was a loud shout from little brother in the bleachers: "You can!...Believe!...Believe!"

Mom was surprised with delight at the little brother's vocal support with these affirmations. And big brother hit a home run. When we believe in others and as others believe in us, there's no telling the rewards or growth that will occur.

A letter to me from Marcia: *I wanted to catch you up on what's been happening. All's well. Very well. No kidding, Bev - When you looked me in the eyes last time I saw you and you told me I had to believe in myself, I experienced* *great love towards me. I decided then and there to believe in myself, and my life is changing dramatically - my business is a business, I am respecting myself, giving myself credit - which is foreign to me. I never really realized that people really like me.*

A lot of the people I meet are searching to regain self-respect, self-worth, and self-confidence. Many have had bad experiences in life and are greatly challenged in letting go of old baggage and old records. My constant encouragement is for them to believe; believe in God, believe in others, and believe in themselves. Believing reverses the negative attitudes, thoughts, and perceptions that have kept them from achieving. It's about daring to accept the challenge to build a new, better life.

We have to learn to accept our disabilities, limitations or physical flaws. The more kindness, compassion, and forgiveness we show toward ourselves, the better off we'll be. And the better able we'll be to understand and appreciate others.

The T-shirt said what? Linda shared an entertaining and enlightening story with me. She was scheduled to attend a Turning Point Retreat some distance from her home. She dreads flying, so her husband, Tom, drove her to the event. When he had to leave early, Linda was stuck and had to fly home by herself. As he departed, she burst into tears and remained tearful the whole day. Her hotel room made her feel worse, so she decided to go out. Linda walked past the hotel gift shop and saw a sign that announced SALE.

She looked and finally found a T-shirt that said across the front: BELIEVE. Because she had just heard me speak about *I can, I will, I believe*, the word resonated in her mind and heart. She purchased the T-shirt.

When she got back to her room, she decided to wear it under her outfit the next day for the closing conference. The event ended, and she had to face her fear of flying home alone. She carried the BELIEVE T-shirt with her on the plane trip. She was fortunate to get an upgrade to first class, sat next to a very nice gentleman, and enjoyed a comfortable flight. Although he looked at her quizzically afterward, they had a great conversation and she told him about buying the T-shirt, then showed it to him.

When she landed and got off the plane, her husband was there to meet her. He asked about her flight and wanted to know what she had done without him at the end of the event. She told him about buying the T-shirt and proudly held it up in front of her.

"See," she said, "it says BELIEVE."

He looked at her with a quizzical expression and said, "Honey, I'm so glad you had a good time, but that shirt does not say BELIEVE. It says BELLEVUE!"

She looked, and sure enough, he was right. She was stunned. Now, when she thinks of that mistake, she finds it amazing, the way God works. To her, that T-shirt will always say BELIEVE.

There is power in believing. Linda so believed that she gained the courage to overcome one of her greatest fears. *I can, I will, I believe...powerful words.*

Carol's comments: This is from a letter I received: *Beverly, your presentation made an indelible impression on me. I believe natural ability is necessary for great endeavors, but listening to your talk, I am reminded of what grit it takes to achieve at an Olympic level. I know I am a strong person, but I forget it sometimes. After hearing your talk, I was motivated and enthused to set goals and to work hard toward achieving them, instead of letting life just happen to me.*

I am paying a lot of attention to your comments on raising children, and have and will pass along ideas to my daughter and son-in-law.

These messages and stories relate personal triumphs and strides toward success by people who are sincerely trying to better themselves...people whose lives I have been invited to touch and influence. Most of the accomplishments may seem small to you, but the personal victories and progress they represent are huge to the person doing the striving. That's the way most people make progress in turning their lives around, with small steps, one at a time. The longest journey starts with a single step.

I get hundreds of cards and letters from people eager to tell me about a personal triumph or a milestone in their progress or simply how they're doing. Many are more dramatic, impressive stories of complete turnaround, incredible new success, and increased personal satisfaction. However, I think it's more fitting to include the smaller stories of success.

People write all the time to thank me for the small role I have played in their steps to success or in their struggles with themselves. And I welcome every message from every one of them. Most do not realize that their thankful notes of progress give me more than I can ever give to them.

CHAPTER 11

Have faith.

As I speak around the country and meet with them face to face, people ask me what I consider the most important aspect of my message. The same question is frequently asked from the audience in our question-and-answer sessions. They seek a shortcut to success... something they can apply immediately that will have an impact on their personal progress.

I generally reply that the points I've made...the components of my methodology...are equally important and necessary to ultimate success. Every attitude, action and recommendation is tied to everything else. They all have to work in unison, like a team, for the individual to reach a higher level of achievement and fulfillment. And that is true.

However, to be perfectly truthful, I do regard one element above the rest, and that is faith. Belief...in yourself, in your own abilities and purpose, and in others...is vital for achievement.

For me personally, faith in God is supremely important. That is why I repeatedly emphasize *believe* in everything I do. Without believing...as without effort or will or purpose or planning...there is no basis for success.

Confidence is the key, and confidence comes from both believing and accomplishing, which generates increased belief and greater accomplishment. That generates momentum which amplifies to give you greater movement toward success and keeps the process going and growing. I have not always been as confident as I am today; it was something I had to learn; and my early successes in athletic competition contributed greatly to the growth of my confidence.

In high school, I ran track and competed in the 110-yard low hurdles. I was one of the top hurdlers in the city. However, a teammate constantly beat me. At almost every meet, she came in first and I came in second. It was challenging, but frustrating, and it didn't help my confidence. I was worried that I would always be second best.

During qualifying for the Alabama state meet, I had injured the quad muscle in my right leg. It was heavily wrapped, and I competed with a nothing-to-lose attitude. The field was very intimidating, full of regional champions. I pushed, and managed to qualify for the state finals in Selma. That was huge for me. I was thrilled and excited to be included at such a high level.

When they called our event, butterflies were busy bobbling around inside me. It was THE BIG TIME, and

I was part of it. My leg was heavily taped. My teammate was in the heat, as well as some of the fastest hurdlers in the state. I shut out everything else and concentrated on what was ahead of me.

The starting gun went off, and I was out of the blocks. All recognition of anyone beside me was gone. I was so focused that all I saw was the next hurdle in front of me. Push/stride...push/stride...over one hurdle after the other until the last hurdle and the sprint for the finish line. I ended up crossing it first and setting a new state record.

I hoped, I prepared, I ignored the injury, I tried, I succeeded. I was the most surprised person at the meet. And it did wonders for my confidence.

I kept going when I faced hurdles and disappointments because I believed I could achieve. I believed that it would get better and that I could overcome the obstacles and do it. There is a saying that is as true in life as it is in athletic competition: *You're not beaten until you think you are.*

Besides confidence, the win gave me hope for my athletic future. I want every one of you to be left with hope. It is essential to faith and such an important component of achieving. Hope helps us orient ourselves to our goals. As we live intentionally and put these goals into perspective day by day, hope energizes us. The more we believe and fix our eyes on our future opportunities and possibilities, the more it influences and shapes our positive actions and potential for success.

In whatever we do to reach our goals and realize our dreams, the true value and lessons are learned in the process. The purpose of the process is to develop an individual attitude that welcomes challenge and seeks out opportunity. It requires facing your failures and refocusing to achieve your desired results. That needs confidence, believing in your gifts and abilities, no matter what. It's about gauging your efforts on a daily basis, accepting your successes and failures in perspective, and resting when the day is done. And moving on to the next day and the next task. And not dwelling on the past.

It's about never giving up, even when you've repeatedly missed your mark. The British Prime Minister and statesman, Winston Churchill, said it best. Toward the end of his career, Churchill, renowned as the greatest orator of his time, was asked to return to his old school, Harrow, where as a student he had almost flunked out. It was anticipated that his speech would instruct and inspire. This is his entire address to the students:

"Young men, never give up. Never give up!
Never give up!! Never, never, never... never...never!"

Churchill succinctly summed up something else that I believe to be true, and it is one of my favorite quotes:

"Success is never final. Failure is never fatal. It is courage that counts."

It takes courage to change your life, and courage stems from confidence and resolve. Faith is the operative quality that ties everything together...and gives you the strength to try and try again. Your beliefs shape your actions. Extended through your lifetime, your actions form your destiny.

I have been fortunate to be part of something great....in my Olympic experience and with Providence. Opportunities came because I pursued them and prepared myself to accept the responsibilities and risks that came with them. I urge you to not be afraid to take risks; start small and grow into the courageous person that you know you are at heart.

I kept the big goal always before me, and learned that the true value came in the daily grind of pursuing the dream. Success really comes ultimately in the effort we give, in striving to be our best. Success = attitude + proficiency. But, because we're human, it's not as simple as a formula and requires more than competence. It's about congruency in heart and action; it involves conviction and caring. It's giving your best so you can be your best for the team, the family, the organization or the company. It's the daily commitment that makes the dream come true.

Do the ordinary with such consistency that you create extraordinary results. Take the first step and the second step to meet the challenge. Face your doubts, fears, and anxieties head-on to achieve your goals.

I understand that I am perceived to be a woman of inner strength, but my own momentary uncertainties and lapses of self-confidence remain issues I have to deal with daily. There are times when I waver or my confidence is eroded. I'm as human as you are, and it isn't easy to stay positive and remain motivated.

There was a time when I considered it a weakness to admit any fear or worry. Because I am such a private person, it was hard to find an an outlet for my doubts, anxieties and concerns. I have learned to share myself with others and communicate these things. In doing so, I have found increased courage and strength.

Venture out of your comfort zone and try something that is difficult, but not impossible for you. You can do it. At first, when I considered speaking in front of people from a stage, it scared me silly.

Brian challenged and encouraged me, and I tried it. I found that I was pretty effective and people listened. It wasn't easy, but it wasn't nearly as difficult or as frightening as I had presumed. And it gave me a chance to reach out and encourage many, many people. The audiences got bigger, and I got a little bit more confident every time I spoke. Now I speak before thousands at nationwide events, and I can really get my message out there. And I enjoy it.

My husband loves to challenge me. This book is a result of his prompting. In my wildest imaginings, I never would have thought I could author a book...but it happened. And God had a hand in it, for sure.

Becoming your best means breaking old, bad habits and generating new, good habits. That takes will power. There is much we must discard, replace, or refine in order to achieve success. Surround yourself with things that motivate and inspire you: friends, mentors, books...positive things that help you to grow and progress.

Remember, I always say: *Dream big and do the ordinary with such consistency that your dreams become reality.* It's about our daily tasks and realizing that success in any endeavor requires that we focus our attention on the task at hand. Do it as well as you can enthusiastically. I am convinced that intentionally committing to these ordinary daily tasks with great consistency pays off in extraordinary results. We need to expect great things. *Expect great things to occur today*...and every day. And maintain that expectation.

Set goals for yourself, and write them down on paper. I have witnessed and experienced first-hand the startling effectiveness of this simple procedure. Make your goals realistic and reachable, but not necessarily small.

From my experience at the 1988 Olympics, I learned a life-transforming lesson about goal-setting. I will instill it in my children and assure that it is passed on to our grandchildren. I will teach our children how significant it is to set goals, and I will encourage them to keep their sights on their GREAT BIG AUDACIOUS GOALS. But I will also make sure they know that true wealth or success in life is found along the way...in the journey, in the process. The reward comes in searching and expecting and working hard at it, as if trying to find a hidden treasure. I will be sure to teach them to celebrate their victories and not miss their rewards and blessings along the way.

Far too often, I overlooked or neglected to celebrate my own lessons learned or victories won. I was too focused on the end and did not find joy in the day. The struggles, the setbacks, the lesser wins along the way, the disappointments...those moments are what make the person, and all those moments reflect a ray of hope.

Hold on to your dreams. Too many times we lose sight of what we really want. Too often we quit on our dreams and hopes because we're afraid to fail...or to succeed. Here is a wonderful story that crystallizes these thoughts for me:

On the 4th of July in 1952, a young woman named Florence Chadwick went into the water off Catalina Island. She had been the first woman to swim the English Channel in both directions, and she intended to swim from Catalina to the California coast.

The Pacific Ocean was numbing cold. The heavy fog was so thick that she couldn't see the boats accompanying her. As she swam, sharks came near and had to be driven away with rifle fire. After 15 hours, she asked to be taken out of the water. Her coach encouraged her to continue because they were close to land, but all Florence could see was fog. This brave woman quit just a half-mile from her goal.

She said later, "If I could have seen the land, I might have made it."

It wasn't fear or exhaustion that caused her to fail; it was the fog. She lost sight of her goal. Two months later, Florence Chadwick tried again. From the same beach, across the same channel, she went the distance and set a new record for it...because she could see her way. I believe my faith helps me see my way with God's light.

Don't be afraid to accept help from others or to let others know you need help and support. Communicate your need clearly. Be specific, open and candid. Most people sense the need in another and are glad to help, but they're not mind readers. *Ask, and you shall receive. Knock, and it shall be opened to you.*

Conversely, be eager and ready to help others, and let them know you are there for them. My achievements and successes didn't spring from me unaided. They came with a lot of help from many others: parents, mentors, coaches, friends and, of course, by God's providence. The help I received makes me want to help others. The more you do for others, the greater the return to yourself, the more you want to do for others. It is a great cycle of good that rewards and refreshes your soul.

In this same regard, you need others in order to be the best that you can be. Cooperate and work with others joyously and openly. Be a team player. Join with others in common goals and efforts. I have always found the team experience to be highly rewarding. My coaches thought me to be very team-oriented. Learn to naturally work with others and promote the spirit of teamwork.

Take the time to review what you've done and measure your progress objectively. Plan ahead. Include time for relaxation and enjoyment of what you've achieved.

At the beginning of each year, Brian and I get away for a while to regroup and re-evaluate and plan for the future. This private time together has proven precious. Not only do we evaluate the previous year and plan for the coming year, we also use the time to heighten our relationship. We make sure we're together in everything important and staying the course in all aspects of our lives. This togetherness creates momentum for our family, our spiritual journey, our personal life, our financial state, and our business affairs.

As I have said before, momentum is an important part of this process of achieving and being successful. Be creative in finding ways and people and things to keep your momentum going. Moving forward toward your goals is a must.

Whenever you need to or want to or have to...whenever you are challenged...say the affirmations. *I can, I will, I believe.* These declarations aid in transforming our attitudes, and they provide a vocal keynote of hope.

When we realize that our very being was designed, put together and knitted into mankind by the Creator; when we understand that each and every one of us has been graced with certain gifts and abilities and a destiny that no other can fulfill; when we accept that no one is excluded...then we begin to think *I can.*

The you that often gets buried under your own false perceptions...or the you that has been put down or cast aside, neglected or rejected by others...resurfaces and comes into the light. That is the you which is so very special and precious...the you that has the capabilities, mentally and spiritually, to achieve greatness. Oh, how special you are. Believe it.

Have faith in yourself and your own abilities and especially in the Lord. At our wedding, all the decorations carried these verses from Proverbs 3:5-3:6. I keep them always in mind.

Trust in the Lord with all your heart,

And do not lean on your own understanding.

In all your ways acknowledge Him,

And He will make your paths straight.

We were traveling with our children in Ireland, taking a tour of Dublin, all sitting up top on a double-decker bus. It came time to exit, and we started down the very steep spiral staircase to get off the bus. Suddenly there was a halt in the procession. Adam was stopped halfway down. To prevent an unloading jam, I rushed to assist him. He shook his head and blurted loudly, "No mommy! *I can, I will, I believe*!"

These affirmations have become a very real part of our little boy's belief system. They simply need to be said and believed to work for you and your children, too.

Take a moment and pretend that I am holding your cheeks, looking into your eyes, and declaring these encouraging words to you. *I can, I will, I believe.* Say them out loud in whatever circumstance you may find yourself. Better yet, try looking in the mirror and saying these affirmations to yourself while you look yourself in the eyes. Still better, try doing this for a few moments every day for the next month, and see their effect. Awesome experiences or transformations may come from it. Use these words throughout your day. And, as Adam demanded, say them like you mean it.

I can, I will, I believe.

Acknowledgements

I thank the following persons for their part in making this book a reality and for their important role in my life:

Brian, my wonderful friend, my encourager and incredibly insightful husband, for his unconditional love and support. Without him, there would not be this book.

Anthony, Anna, Alex, Adam, Amy and Alysha, our children, for the sheer joy they bring to my life.

James and Julia Robinson, my father and mother, who have been my biggest fans since day one of my life.

Carolyn and Stacey, my sisters, for their continuing love and support.

Therese and George Buffini and all my brothers-in-law: Gary, John, Dermot, and Kevin, and Louise Robinson, my sister-in-law, for their warm and unconditional acceptance of me.

Bob Bertucci, my coach at the University of Tennessee, who pushed me to excel and opened my eyes to a bigger world.

Joan Cronan, the Athletic Director at Tennessee, who believed in me and provides great opportunity to all the female athletes in the Lady Vol athletic program.

Linda Sale and Patty Guthrie, who faithfully prayed for me and this book's production.

The passionate people of Providence Systems who keep the vision alive and to all those clients who encouraged me to believe.

Mort Keilty for his help, patience and craft with all aspects of this book.

To order, copy this page and send it in.

To order additional copies of the book:

I can, I will, I believe is available at special quantity discounts for bulk purchases for sales promotions, premiums or educational use.
Special books or book excerpts also can be created to fit specific needs.
For details, write: **Providence Systems, Inc.,**
        6349 Palomar Oaks Court, Carlsbad, CA 92009
ISBN 0-9715638-4-5   **$19.95** U.S.

Payable in U.S. funds only. Postage & handling: U.S./Can. $5.00 for one book, $1.00 for each additional book. International: $8.00 for one book, $1.00 for each additional book. We accept Visa, MC, AMEX, Discover, checks ($15.00 fee for returned checks) and money orders. No cash/COD. Call 800-945-3485 or mail your orders to:
Providence Systems, Inc., 6349 Palomar Oaks Court, Carlsbad, CA 92009

Bill my credit card _____exp. _____

Visa _____ MC _____ AMEX _____ Discover_____

Signature_____

Bill to _____ Book Total $_____

Address _____

City _____ST ____ZIP _____   Applicable sales tax $ _____

Phone No. _____   Postage & handling $ _____

Ship to: _____

Address _____   Total amount due $ _____

City _____ST ____ZIP _____

Please allow 4-6 weeks for U.S. delivery. International orders allow 6-8 weeks.
This offer is subject to change without notice.